DREAM BIG

HEROES WHO DARED TO BE BOLD

SALLY MORGAN

■SCHOLASTIC

Scholastic Children's Books,
Euston House,
24 Eversholt Street,
London NW1 1DB, UK

A division of Scholastic Ltd
London ~ New York ~ Toronto ~ Sydney ~ Auckland
Mexico City ~ New Delhi ~ Hong Kong

First published in the UK by Scholastic Ltd, 2019

Text by Sally Morgan © Scholastic Children's Books
Illustrations by James Rey Sanchez © Scholastic Children's Books

ISBN 978 1407 18903 1

Printed and bound in the UK by Bell and Bain Ltd, Glasgow

2 4 6 8 10 9 7 5 3 1

The right of Sally Morgan and James Rey Sanchez to be identified as the
author and illustrator of this work respectively has been asserted by them
in accordance with the Copyright, Designs and Patents Act, 1988.

Papers used by Scholastic Children's Books are made from wood grown in
sustainable forests.

www.scholastic.co.uk

CONTENTS

INTRODUCTION

In this book you will find the stories of one hundred people who dared to dream big dreams and then did something to achieve those dreams. That doesn't mean the people in this book didn't come up against obstacles. It doesn't mean they weren't terrified that they might fall flat on their faces. It doesn't even mean any of them were super-popular, perfect people – nobody is. Some of these people did big things, some did small things but they all did something to change their lives and often the lives of countless others. After each entry, you will discover a way to transform your dreams from something you have, into something you do.

Unlike dreams, books (even big ones) have limits. One hundred people sounds like a lot, but it isn't at all. All of the beautiful, wonderful human-made things we have in the world today are the result of many, many more **BIG DREAMERS**.

Make your big dreams more than something you have – make them something you do.

DREAM BIG.
DO SOMETHING.
CHANGE YOUR WORLD.

Adwoa Aboah

BRITISH

"Mental health isn't all of me but it's a massive part of my journey and a massive part of my whole being. Having got through it – it's 100% my responsibility to use it for something bigger and to be one of many voices for people who might not have someone to talk to or understand what's going on."

1992 –
Model | Actress | Campaigner

Adwoa Aboah was born in London and was a very happy little girl. That changed when, aged thirteen, Adwoa went to boarding school. Surrounded by girls with lighter skin, Adwoa felt she didn't fit in and that everyone else was more beautiful. She was wrong. At sixteen, Adwoa signed with Storm model agency. On the surface, Adwoa had everything a girl could wish for. She went to a good school, had supportive parents and a successful modelling career, yet she was still very unhappy. The privilege she had grown up with made her feel like she had no right to feel the way she did so she kept quiet.

As Adwoa got older her struggles worsened. She became anxious and depressed and used illegal drugs to make herself feel better. They did not work. Feeling she had nowhere to turn Adwoa tried to take her own life. Thankfully she did not succeed. Instead, once she was well enough, Adwoa travelled to Arizona, US, where she entered rehab. While in rehab, Adwoa had a lot of therapy. When she returned home she used what she had learned to create Gurls Talk – a safe space where girls just like Adwoa can confide in one another about the issues that affect their lives.

Adwoa may not be a trained psychologist, but she speaks from experience. She saw a need for girls to be able to express themselves openly. Her honesty inspires girls from all over the world to share their own experiences and support each other through them.

One thing you can do: find your community. If you don't fit into one, build one yourself.

1983 –
Rapper | Writer | Historian

Akala was born in Sussex, UK. His father left before he was born and he was raised by his mother and sister.

Growing up, Akala was a talented football player. He was selected to play for Wimbledon and West Ham youth teams. When not playing football, Akala loved to read and loved to learn. Akala worked hard at school and did well at his studies, but in spite of this he was placed in a group for students with additional educational needs because he was deemed 'too bright for a working-class brown boy'.

When Akala was ten his mother became ill and his sister looked after him. Despite his mother's illness and how he was treated at school, Akala just got smarter and more creative. He gave up football to pursue another passion – music. Observing what was happening around him and using what he learned, Akala wrote songs and poetry. He released his first hip hop album, *It's Not a Rumour*, in May 2006.

Akala's music is very different to a lot of commercial hip hop, which is about love, money and greed. Akala uses his music as a platform to shine a light on political injustice such as structural racism, and also to highlight problems in the British education system and music industry.

His way with words has also led him to write a bestselling history book and earned him an honorary doctorate.

One thing you can do: politics affects everyone – be yourself and speak out when you think things are unfair.

Akala
(Kingslee James Daley)

BRITISH

*When asked whether he would ever get into politics

"I can't say never, but there are millions of ways to engage in politics that may be more productive. Having a generation of young working-class kids that aspire to be clever more than they aspire to the things that society has told them to aspire to, that's political."*

Alan Turing

BRITISH

"Sometimes it is the people no one can imagine anything of who do the things no one can imagine."

Mathematician | Computer Scientist

When Alan Turing was a boy he had a passion for maths and science. He was so determined to get a good education, that when a strike meant he was unable to catch a bus to his first day at boarding school, he got on his bike and cycled sixty miles to get there.

During World War Two, Alan worked for the British government at a place called Bletchley Park. There he led a team attempting to decipher coded enemy messages. Alan's maths and logic helped him to develop a machine which was able to crack the German's 'Enigma' code and reveal their plans. Many believe his work shortened the war by as much as two years and saved countless lives.

In 1952, Alan was found guilty of being a homosexual, which was a crime in Britain at the time. Instead of going to prison, he agreed to go on medication that would leave him sick and suffering from depression, which led to his death.

In 2013, more than sixty years after his conviction, Alan was granted a royal pardon, which led to many other similar convictions being overturned.

Today, Alan is remembered as a hero – the father of modern computing and one of the greatest minds of his age.

One thing you can do: learn to code. Coders are building the world of the future. What do you think it should look like?

1985 –
Lawyer | Activist | Prison Reformer

Growing up, Alexander McLean loved school and loved to learn. He had lots of interests and was fascinated by civil rights leaders such as Martin Luther King Jr and Nelson Mandela (see page 160).

Throughout his teenage years, Alexander volunteered for several charities, helping to care for people with disabilities.

When he was sixteen, Alexander read an article that would change his life. It was about Dr Anne Merriman, a former nun from Liverpool, who had set up a hospice in Uganda. Inspired by her work, he wrote to the hospice and asked if he could work for them, but they wrote back to say he was too young. But Alexander didn't give up. He wrote again and eventually showed up on their doorstep.

In Uganda, Alexander worked at Mulago Hospital where he met many prisoners who received little food or medicine. Alexander visited their prisons and set about trying to change things for the inmates, many of whom had been wrongly convicted. He raised money to improve conditions and to help prisoners gain access to legal representation. He began educating prisoners so they could represent themselves in court, founding the world's first prison-based law school.

Alexander also set up a charity called the African Prisons Project. It is estimated that over 3,000 people have been released from prison in Uganda and Kenya thanks to his work.

> **One thing you can do:** volunteer your time. Giving your time to serve others can change their lives and your own for the better.

Alexander McLean

BRITISH

"The law is here to serve all of us. We want to see people getting out of prison, becoming lawyers and judges, and politicians, and legal academics, and business leaders, going from the margins of society to the centre of it."

Amelia Earhart

AMERICAN

"Everyone has oceans to fly, if they have the heart to do it. Is it reckless? Maybe. But what do dreams know of boundaries?"

1897 – (declared dead 5 January 1939)
Aviator | Writer | Activist

When **Amelia Earhart** was a girl, few women led adventurous lives or had exciting careers. Any that did were likely to end up in Amelia's scrapbook, where she kept newspaper clippings of all the women who inspired her. Amelia was determined that one day she would be one of these adventurous women, but it wasn't until she took her first flight in an aeroplane in 1920 that she knew how. She was going to fly. But flying was expensive.

Amelia worked hard and saved up money from her various jobs. She even borrowed money from her mother to pay for flying lessons, eventually buying her own yellow plane, *The Canary*.

Once she had her pilot's licence, there was no stopping Amelia. She was the first woman to fly to an altitude of 14,000 feet (4,267 metres), the first woman to fly across the Atlantic, the first woman to fly coast to coast across the United States and the first woman to fly solo from Hawaii to the US mainland across the Pacific Ocean.

Amelia's daring feats captured the imaginations of people all over the world – but she had one more epic journey that she wanted to make. Determined to be the first woman to fly around the world, on 1 June 1937 Amelia embarked on what would be the beginning of her last adventure. After a number of successful flights, Amelia took off in New Guinea on 2 July – never to be seen again.

One thing you can do: keep a scrapbook of people that inspire you and look for ways you can inspire others.

1999 –
Activist

In April 2017, eighteen-year-old student Amika George read an article that would change her life and set her on the path of improving the lives of countless other women and girls around the world. This article was about how some girls from low-income families in the United Kingdom weren't able to afford sanitary protection items, such as tampons and pads, and how this left them feeling humiliated and even unable to attend school.

Amika was horrified by what she read, so that afternoon she started her #freeperiod campaign. Through the power of social media she is now the head of a global army fighting to break the stigma surrounding menstruation and help the millions of women across the world affected by period poverty.

In December 2017, Amika and her organization led a protest to 10 Downing Street to demand that Prime Minister Theresa May and the UK government 'provide free menstruation products for all girls already on free school meals'.

In March 2018, Amika's organization was awarded £1.5 million by the UK government to help to start tackling the problem.

One thing you can do: find your cause. Read the news to find out what in the world you want to make better for people and then demand it happens on social media.

Amika George

BRITISH

"Unless we break the stigma and normalise conversation around menstruation, we will never accept that periods make women incredible and our bodies powerful."

Aneurin Bevan

BRITISH

"Discontent arises from a knowledge of the possible, as contrasted with the actual."

1897 – 1960
Politician | Activist

Like a lot of children in poor working-class families at the time, Aneurin Bevan left school when he was just thirteen years old to work at the local coal mine. Work at the mine was low paid, difficult and dangerous. As the years went by, Aneurin became more and more involved in campaigning for worker's rights.

In 1926, mine owners were preparing to reduce the already low pay of miners and increase their working hours. The miners were upset by this, as were workers in lots of other industries, believing that if miners could be treated this way, anybody could. On 4 May 1926, about 1.5 million workers, including bus drivers, printers and steelworkers, didn't go to work. This was called a general strike and Aneurin was one of its leaders in South Wales. The country ground to a halt. However, after nine days, most people were forced back to work.

In spite of the general strike not achieving its goals, people noticed Aneurin's commitment to improving the lives of working people and he was elected to parliament in 1929 as Labour MP for Ebbw Vale.

In 1945, Aneurin was appointed Minister of Health. He had grown up seeing the health problems poverty could cause and now he was in a position to do something about it. In 1948, under Aneurin's guidance, the British government took control of medical services in the United Kingdom. They promised free healthcare for all and established what we now call the National Health Service (NHS).

One thing you can do: believe in change. When you see something that is unfair, find a group of friends who agree with you and do what you can to change it.

1958 – 2006
Journalist | Human Rights Activist

Anna Politkovskaya was the daughter of Soviet diplomats. She grew up in New York, far away from the troubles in her parent's homeland, the communist Soviet Union. Anna described herself as somewhat of a 'swot' and earned a place at Moscow State University to study journalism.

In the 1990s, Anna reported from Chechnya, where there was fierce fighting between the Russian government and a group of people who wanted Chechnya to be an independent country. Anna proved what a fearless journalist she was, risking her life to report on the terrible things done by both sides.

Anna's stories made her unpopular with the Russian government. In 2001, she was arrested by the authorities, who claimed she was a spy. The following year, a packed theatre in Moscow was seized by armed Chechens and over 800 of the people inside were taken hostage. Anna risked her life negotiating with the leader to try and get the hostages released.

When a group of children were taken hostage in 2004, Anna flew in to cover the story – but she was poisoned while in the air. After Anna recovered, she went back to work risking her life to write the truth.

Anna was found dead on the 7 October 2006, the day she had planned to publish a story criticizing the Chechen Prime Minister Ramzan Kadyrov. Many believe she was assassinated by the Russian government.

> **One thing you can do:** write about issues in your community that you think should be highlighted.

Anna Politkovskaya

RUSSIAN

"How we react to the tragedy of one small person accurately reflects our attitude towards a whole nationality, and increasing the numbers doesn't change much."

Anne Frank

GERMAN

"How wonderful it is that nobody need wait a single moment before starting to improve the world." (English translation)

1929 – 1945
Diarist | Refugee

Anne Frank was born in Frankfurt, Germany. She was a lively Jewish girl who dreamed of one day being a famous writer.

In 1933, Adolf Hitler became the leader of Germany. Hitler blamed the Jewish people for many of the country's problems. With Hitler as leader, life for Jewish people became very dangerous. Many left Germany to seek refuge in other countries. In 1934, Anne joined her family, who had moved to Amsterdam in the Netherlands the previous year.

In 1940, Hitler's army invaded the Netherlands. The Franks went into hiding in rooms concealed behind a bookcase in a building near where Otto Frank, Anne's father, worked. They stayed there for two years. Anne kept a detailed diary of the events during her time in hiding, as well as her hopes and dreams for the future.

The Frank family remained hidden until August 1944 when German soldiers discovered their hiding place. The family were separated from one another and sent to concentration camps. Many millions of people were killed in these camps, including six million Jewish people.

Anne and her sister Margot died of a disease called typhus in Bergen-Belsen camp, just one month before Allied forces liberated the camp. Otto was the only member of the Frank family to survive. He returned to Amsterdam where he discovered his daughter's diary.

Today, the rooms where Anne and her family hid are a museum and her diary has been translated into over seventy languages.

One thing you can do: keep a journal or a blog. It will be fascinating to look back on your memories one day.

1966 –
Engineer | Businesswoman | Spaceflight Participant

Ever since Anousheh Ansari was a girl, growing up in Iran, she would look at the stars and dream of one day becoming a space explorer.

When Anousheh was a teenager, her family left Iran to move to the United States. This was difficult for Anousheh, who at the time could not speak English. But Anousheh was determined – she quickly learned the language and worked hard at school, going on to earn a place at university. There she studied electronics and computer engineering and used her skills to start her own communication software company.

Anousheh became a successful businesswoman, but she never forgot her dream of one day going to space. She was now in a position to make it happen. On 18 September 2006, Anousheh's dream came true when she travelled to the International Space Station as part of a commercial space flight. The flight was expensive, but Anousheh believed it was worth every penny.

In 2017, Anousheh accepted an Oscar on behalf of an Iranian film director, Asghar Farhadi. She used her speech to protest against the inhumane treatment of immigrants from Muslim countries by US President Donald Trump.

One thing you can do: never forget your dreams. If life takes you in a different direction, look for the path to lead you back where you want to go.

Anousheh Ansari

IRANIAN-AMERICAN

"I hope to inspire everyone – especially young people, women and young girls all over the world, and in Middle Eastern countries that do not provide women with the same opportunities as men – to not give up their dreams and to pursue them."

April Ashley

BRITISH

"I knew from the age dot that I was a girl.
My only dreams were about growing up
to be a woman."

1935 –
Activist | Model

April Ashley was born in Liverpool as George Jamieson. From a young age, April knew she was different from the boys in her class. As she grew up, she felt more and more like a girl, but April's classmates couldn't accept her differences and so she was badly bullied.

When April was around fifteen, she decided to get away and joined the navy. But life at sea was hard and April became so unhappy that she tried to take her own life. Fortunately, she didn't succeed and instead was discharged. But April knew something needed to change.

April moved to London and began living as a woman. In 1960, April travelled to Casablanca, Morocco, to become one of the very first people to have gender reassignment surgery.

April always knew she was a woman, but her birth certificate still said she was male. April never gave up. She wrote to the government to have her gender officially recognized in the hope that this would lead the way for a change in the law for all transgender people. After much campaigning, the Gender Recognition Act was passed, and in 2005 April Ashley was issued with a new birth certificate confirming what she had known all her life.

In 2012, April Ashley was awarded an MBE in recognition for her work for transgender equality.

> **One thing you can do:** try to include everyone in your friendship group and if you see anyone being excluded or bullied, speak to a responsible adult.

1961 –
Politician | 44th President of the United States

Barack Obama was born in Honolulu, Hawaii, US, and didn't have an easy childhood. His parents divorced when he was young. Barack lived with his mother in Washington State then in Indonesia until he moved back to Hawaii to live with his grandparents.

Despite all of this moving around, Barack worked hard at school and went to university in Los Angeles and then Columbia University, New York.

After graduating, Barack moved to Chicago where he worked for an organization that supported people who had lost their jobs. While there, Barack became interested in studying law and went on to study at Harvard. He began practising at a law firm that represented people who were victims of discrimination. Barack was working to make people's lives better, but he knew if he was going to change the lives of more people, he would have to get into politics.

In 1996, Barack was elected to the Illinois State Senate and in 2005 he was elected to the US Senate, representing Illinois. As a senator, he became known as a powerful speaker.

In February 2007, Barack announced he was running for president and in 2008 he was elected as the 44th President of the United States. As president, he sought to make healthcare more affordable and spoke out about gun control and human rights.

> **One thing you can do:** be the change you want to see. No matter how small, do something to make someone else's life better.

Barack Obama

AMERICAN

"Change will not come if we wait for some other person or if we wait for some other time. We are the ones we've been waiting for. We are the change that we seek."

Befeqadu Hailu

ETHIOPIAN

"I believe that I am in a struggle. I am challenging the organized system of government whom I believe are criminals. I want to be part of history in changing that ugly fact."

1980 –
Writer | Blogger | Activist

Ethiopian IT consultant and writer Befeqadu Hailu was arrested in April 2014. He was accused of 'intending to destabilize the nation' and sentenced to a prison term. Befeqadu spent more than a year in jail for terrorism charges for his links to a group he co-founded called Zone9. The group weren't terrorists, but bloggers who hoped to start young people talking about a democratic future for Ethiopia. A future in which people could speak freely about politics, in which human rights were respected and where a government was democratically elected.

Ethiopians had hoped to have their first truly democratic election in 2005, but many believe the ruling party rigged the election in their favour. After the election, demonstrations against the results were banned and supporters of the opposition party were attacked. Since then, people criticizing the government have been labelled terrorists and arrested.

Befeqadu was released in October 2015 and absolved of charges of terrorism but was rearrested just over a year later for giving an interview on an international radio station. He was beaten and humiliated in prison and forced to promise never to write again but to this day, Befeqadu is determined that, despite the dangers, he will continue to fight for democracy and freedom of speech in the country that he loves.

One thing you can do: never take your ability to vote in democratic elections for granted. Educate yourself about the political parties you will be able to vote for so that you are ready to make your voice heard when the time comes. If you are fourteen or over, consider joining the party that most reflects your beliefs.

1996 –
Athlete

When Bethany Firth was a small child she fell into a swimming pool. This made Bethany terrified of the water and determined never to swim.

That was until Bethany went to a school where swimming lessons were compulsory. Bethany did everything she could to get out of lessons, like pretending to have forgotten her swimsuit when she had left it out of her bag on purpose.

Eventually, Bethany couldn't avoid swimming lessons any longer – she had to get into the water. But once she started swimming, she never looked back. She trained regularly and became a strong swimmer, going on to represent Great Britain in the 2012 London Paralympics. She won gold in the 100 metres backstroke S14 category for swimmers with an intellectual impairment. Bethany has a learning difficulty that causes short-term memory loss.

After her success in London, Bethany continued to train hard and when it was time for her to compete in the 2016 Rio Paralympics she hoped she was ready, this time competing for Team GB.

Bethany returned home triumphant having won more medals than any other British athlete in the games – three golds and a silver. In 2017, Bethany was invited to Buckingham Palace to receive an MBE for her services to swimming.

> **One thing you can do:** don't let fear stop you from trying new things.

Bethany Firth

NORTHERN IRISH

"I feel like sport has opened so many doors for me.
I'm delighted to [...] share my story and help inspire
people to achieve their dreams. I also want to help
people get a better understanding of people with
learning disability."

Beyonce
(Beyonce Knowles-Carter)

AMERICAN

"Your self-worth is determined by you. You don't have to depend on someone telling you who you are."

1981 –
Singer | Songwriter | Businesswoman

Growing up, Beyoncé didn't always love to be the centre of attention. She was shy. When she was seven, her mother signed her up for dance lessons, hoping it would give her more confidence and help her to make some new friends. It worked. Beyoncé was a natural entertainer who loved to perform. She entered local talent competitions and won. This was just the beginning.

Beyoncé made friends too. She formed a group called Girl Tyme. Beyoncé and the group worked hard touring and playing gigs until 1997 when they landed a major record deal and renamed the band Destiny's Child.

Beyoncé loved performing in Destiny's Child and they became one of the most popular groups on the planet – but she still wanted more. She wanted to be a superstar. In 2003, while still a member of the band, Beyoncé released her own album, *Dangerously in Love*. It was a huge success and sold over eleven million copies worldwide. She released one more album with Destiny's Child and then put all of her energy into her solo career. She has since starred in movies, won shelves full of awards and toured the world. Beyoncé is now one of the highest earning musical performers of all time.

Beyoncé worked hard and never gave up on her dream. She is a symbol to millions of girls around the world that they too are powerful and important.

One thing you can do: decide the kind of person you want to be and then be it. Don't let anyone tell you you're not a superstar.

1943 –
Tennis Player | Activist

Billie Jean King was a total natural at sports – her mother was a brilliant swimmer and her father excelled at baseball and basketball. When Billie turned eleven she discovered tennis, but she didn't have her own racket, so she saved up her money to buy one.

By 1961, Billie was ready for Wimbledon. Along with her partner, Karen Hantze, Billie won the women's doubles event. In 1966, Billie won the women's singles championship at Wimbledon, then again in 1967. There was no stopping her.

Billie won tournament after tournament, becoming the first woman to earn more than $100,000 from the game in a single year. She was winning the same championships as the men, but she was winning a fraction of the prize money and thought this was very unfair. Billie used the same determination she used on the court to campaign for the right of women tennis players to compete for the same prize money as men.

In 1975, Billie began to transition from playing professional tennis to coaching, commentating and campaigning for equal opportunities for women in sport.

One thing you can do: speak out about the gender pay gap. A large amount of UK companies pay men more than women by an average of 10%.

Billie Jean King

AMERICAN

"Champions keep playing until they get it right."

Chase Johnsey

AMERICAN

"I think ballet is possibility, ballet is not woman. A great ballerina is able to take a 200-year-old ballet and breathe new life into it. Who knows who's going to have that talent?"

1981 –
Ballet Dancer

Chase Johnsey started ballet lessons at fourteen. He loved ballet, but he was smaller than the other male dancers and was warned he wasn't likely to dance the heroic male roles, leaping and lifting the female ballet dancers across the stage. This didn't bother Chase, as he dreamed of dancing the female roles himself, like Sleeping Beauty, Giselle and Juliet. To make his dream come true he secretly taught himself to dance in pointe shoes, traditionally worn by female ballet dancers.

Chase taught himself well, and at seventeen he joined Les Ballets Trockadero de Monte Carlo, an all-male dance troupe who performed comedic ballets. With the Trocks, Chase was able to tour the world dancing some of the roles he had always dreamed of.

Chase did so well that he won the 2016 Best Male Dancer award at the National Dance Awards in London. In January 2018, Chase left the Trocks and believed his dance career to be over – until the English National Ballet (ENB) invited him to join the company.

At the ENB, Chase practises with the female ballet dancers, working on his pointe technique and strength exercises. Most dancers dream of principal roles, but Chase has already danced many of these. His dream now is to dance in corps – in line with other female ballet dancers – and to have nobody comment about it.

> **One thing you can do:** be open and accepting of people, and avoid making assumptions.

1977 –
Writer | Public Speaker | Activist

Chimamanda Ngozi Adichie was born
into an Igbo family in Enugu, Nigeria. The Igbo people are one of
the largest ethnic groups in Africa. Chimamanda grew up in a house
where the famous writer, Chinua Achebe, had once lived. Chinua
Achebe was Igbo, just like Chimamanda, and when she read his work,
she realized that people who looked like her could be represented in
great writing and even become great writers.

After school, Chimamanda went to university to study to become a
doctor. While there she edited a university magazine and discovered
her love for writing. At nineteen, Chimamanda left Nigeria after
winning a scholarship to study in the US.

The United States was very different to Nigeria. In the US,
people defined her by the colour of her skin rather than who she
was as a person. Chimamanda began writing about her experiences,
giving a voice to African people living in the US.

Chimamanda has written about growing up in Nigeria, and the civil
war that tore the nation apart, as well as writing about being a woman
and why everyone should be a feminist. She now lives in both the US
and Nigeria and tours the world talking about her books that have
characters that look just like her.

> **One thing you can do:** look for people like you
> in books, and if you don't find people like you,
> start writing your own stories.

Chimamanda Ngozi Adichie

NIGERIAN

"I think of myself as a storyteller, but I would not mind at all if someone were to think of me as a feminist writer [...] I'm very feminist in the way I look at the world, and that world view must somehow be part of my work."

Daniel Barenboim

ARGENTINIAN

"I'm not a politician. I'm a conductor.
And therefore, I do what I feel I can do."

1942 –
Orchestra Conductor | Pianist

When five-year-old Daniel Barenboim took his first piano lesson with his mother in Buenos Aires, Argentina, he could not have known that he was beginning a career that would take him all over the world. Daniel learned quickly and by the age of ten he performed his first international concert in Vienna, Austria. Daniel was talented and the music world had started to take notice.

During World War Two, the Nazis murdered over six million Jewish people. After the war ended, many people believed that the Jewish people needed a land of their own, and so Israel was founded. Britain occupied an area of the Middle East known as Palestine and split the land in two, giving one part to the Muslim people that lived there and the other to the Jewish people. Israelis and Palestinians have fought bitterly over this split ever since. In 1952, Daniel's family settled in Israel.

In orchestras, people forget their differences as they join together to make beautiful music. With this in mind, Daniel co-founded the West–Eastern Divan Orchestra with young musicians from all over the Middle East, including Israel and Palestine, to perform together. He even opened a music school for young Palestinians.

Many people disagree with Palestinian musicians working with a Jewish conductor. But that does not stop him. Daniel's musical talent has given him a platform that he uses to bring people together.

One thing you can do: use your talent for good. Whether you are good at music, sport, maths or listening to others, use your talent to bring people together.

1926 –
Naturalist | Broadcaster

David Attenborough, like many people, loved to explore when he was a child. He would collect fossils and natural specimens that he picked up while he was out and about. Unlike most people, he never stopped.

After university, David got a job in television even though, like most people in Great Britain at the time, his family didn't own one. Not having a television didn't stop David. He wanted to make programmes to show people who had never travelled what the world was like.

David worked hard and in 1965 he was promoted to controller of BBC 2, scheduling new programmes. However, commissioning television programmes wasn't his passion, so he left his job and went back to doing what he loved best – exploring the globe and making documentaries about his first love, the natural world.

David's nature documentaries have given generations of people across the globe a love of the natural world. Today, he campaigns to protect endangered species and habitats and works with a number of wildlife charities.

One thing you can do: protect the world's habitats by recycling plastics, avoiding products containing palm oil and cleaning up rubbish in your area.

David Attenborough

BRITISH

"If we [humans] disappeared overnight,
the world would probably be better off."

David Lammy

BRITISH

"Let me speak frankly: separate but equal is a fraud. It is the language that tried to push Rosa Parks to the back of the bus. It is the motif that determined that black and white people could not possibly drink from the same water fountain, eat at the same table or use the same toilets."

1972 –
Politician | Activist

Growing up, David Lammy's greatest worry was that he'd end up in prison. His father left when he was twelve and his mother had to take on three jobs at a time to support her five children. David had friends who had turned to crime after being denied work because of the colour of their skin or where they lived. Life didn't seem very fair.

But David was a talented singer – so gifted that he was offered a scholarship to a choral school in Peterborough. Here, David worked really hard, and then went on to study law at university. He was the first black Briton to attend Harvard Law School. He loved travelling and his work placements took him all over the world, from Jamaica to Thailand.

But although David knew he was helping to fight injustice as a lawyer, he wanted to do it on a bigger scale. He returned to London to pursue a career in politics and was elected as the Labour MP for Tottenham in 2000 aged just twenty-seven.

David's anger at the unfairness he saw growing up has a big impact on his views. From condemning the Grenfell Tower fire to speaking out about the Windrush scandal, David uses his voice to fight for the most vulnerable people in society.

One thing you can do: ask the questions that nobody else is willing to ask, even if that means challenging your friends when they are being unjust or unkind.

1970 –
Historian | Broadcaster

Born in Lagos, to a white British mother and a black Nigerian father, David Olusoga grew up in Newcastle, where there were very few black or mixed-race people at the time. David experienced racism while growing up, and describes being spat at by white men when he was a boy and having a brick thrown through the window of his home. Things became so bad that his family had to have police protection.

David's mother encouraged him to study hard as school, which he did – studying history and journalism at university before taking a job with the BBC. At the BBC he makes documentaries that attempt to fill in the gaps in the history lessons British children have been taught for decades.

In his documentaries, David demonstrates that the British Empire profited heavily from the trade and labour of enslaved people of colour and that, far from being a recent phenomenon, people of colour have been shaping the nation's history since Roman times.

David writes for newspapers and magazines, and has penned several award-winning books, ensuring that the story of black British history is told.

One thing you can do: learn about the history of Britain and the British Empire. Delve deeper to discover the contributions of minority groups.

David Olusoga

BRITISH-NIGERIAN

"Black history is a series of missing chapters from British history, I'm trying to put those bits back in."

Desmond Tutu

SOUTH AFRICAN

"Do your little bit of good where you are;
it's those little bits of good put together that
overwhelm the world."

1931 –
Minister | Human Rights Activist

When Desmond Tutu was growing up in South Africa it was a country in turmoil because of a system known as 'apartheid'. Apartheid was a set of laws the white-run government of South Africa had put in place to divide people based on the colour of their skin, making it illegal for people of colour to live or work in 'white' areas.

As a boy, Desmond wanted to be a doctor, but he didn't have enough money to go to medical school. Instead he became a teacher and eventually a minister in the Anglican Church.

Desmond was an excellent minister – he spoke out against the cruelty and unfairness of apartheid. His speeches drew international attention and he went on to win the Nobel Peace Prize in 1984. This attention put pressure on the South African government already struggling with violent protests inside the country.

In 1994, Nelson Mandela became the first black president of South Africa. Desmond was made head of the Truth and Reconciliation Commission, a group set up to look into the terrible crimes committed during apartheid. The aim of the commission was to record these crimes accurately and compensate those affected, rather than to punish the perpetrators, bringing people together instead of pushing them further apart. It was considered a revolutionary way to resolve conflict and bring about peace.

> **One thing you can do:** do your bit, no matter how small. Do something to help someone else or make the world a better place.

1937 – 2014
Writer | First Nations Activist

When Doris Pilkington was born in Western Australia, her parents named her Nugi, but she was not allowed to keep that name. The white owner of the land her family lived on insisted she was named 'Doris'.

When she was young, Doris was taken from her home and forced to live in a camp for people of Aboriginal or mixed descent. Her mother escaped with her baby sister but she had to leave Doris behind.

Christian missionaries at the camp taught Doris that she should be ashamed of her dark skin and Aboriginal heritage. The Department of Native Affairs wanted to wipe out the Aboriginal people by raising mixed heritage children to hate the culture of their parents.

In 1962, twenty-one years after they were separated, Doris and her mother were reunited. Doris discovered that when her mother was just fourteen years old she had escaped from a camp with her younger sister and cousin. Together they made a daring journey of over 1,000 miles on foot, following a rabbit-proof fence to find their way home. Doris went on to write a bestselling book inspired by her mother's story. The book and film of *Follow the Rabbit-Proof Fence* drew global attention to a dark period in Australia's history.

The Australian government's policy of taking indigenous and mixed-race children from their families continued into the 1970s. In 2008, the government apologized to these 'stolen generations'.

> **One thing you can do:** discover the stories of First Nation writers by reading books like *Follow the Rabbit-Proof Fence* by Doris Pilkington.

Doris Pilkington Garimara

AUSTRALIAN

The entire Aboriginal population grew to realize what
the arrival of the European settlers meant for them:
it was the destruction of their traditional society
and the dispossession of their lands."

Eddie Izzard

BRITISH

"It seems to me people are always capable of being either brave and curious or fearful and suspicious. If you track humanity all the way through, the periods of success for civilisation are those periods where we have been brave and curious."

1962 –
Comedian | Actor | Political Activist

Eddie Izzard moved around a lot when he was little. Born in what is now Yemen to British parents, he then spent time living in Northern Ireland and Wales. When Eddie was six, his mother died. Eddie was completely heartbroken. He and his older brother built a huge model railway to try and take their minds off their sadness, but the pain never really went away.

Eddie always knew he had both a boy mode and a girl mode but felt under pressure to hide this. At boarding school, he loved taking part in plays, though he rarely got a starring role. As a young man, he decided to leave university to try his hand at street performance and discovered a talent for stand-up comedy. Eddie started publicly wearing dresses, high heels and make-up, and in 1985 he came out as transgender. He was ready to show the world who he really was.

Eddie is now a successful comedian, but his achievements don't stop there. He's won roles in films, learned lots of different languages and spoken out on political issues. He's also run numerous marathons, raising an enormous amount of money for charity – including running twenty-seven marathons in twenty-seven days for Sport Relief. His openness and bravery have encouraged others around the world to embrace their differences.

One thing you can do: raise some money for a good cause – you could run a race, hold a bake sale or take part in a sponsored silence.

1915 – 2011
Writer | Poet | Human Rights Campaigner

Emanuel Litvinoff was born in East London to Russian Jewish parents. His family had fled the city of Odessa, in present-day Ukraine after anti-Semitic attacks (called 'pogroms') threatened the lives of the Jewish people there. The Litvinoffs were very poor. In 1917, Emanuel's father left to fight in the Russian Revolution, but never returned home.

At school, Emanuel experienced racist bullying and after failing at his exams and being picked on to fight other boys at school, he eventually found himself homeless.

When war broke out in 1939, Emanuel did not want to fight, but when he discovered more about what was happening to Jewish people across Europe he signed up to serve in the military. While in the army, Emanuel began publishing his poems and became known as a war poet. After the war he continued to write, using his work to campaign against anti-Semitism.

On a visit to Moscow in 1956, Emanuel witnessed first-hand how Soviet policies were making life impossible for Jewish people. Emanuel believed more could have been done to prevent the horrors experienced by Jewish people during World War Two and was determined that this would not happen again. He started a campaign to allow people of Jewish descent to emigrate to the US and Israel. It worked and today it is believed that thousands of Jewish people in Israel and the US owe their freedom to Litvinoff.

One thing you can do: watch what you read. Look out for persecution and discrimination hidden in great writing, from Shylock in Shakespeare, to Fagin in Dickens, to present-day works.

Emanuel Litvinoff

BRITISH

"One thought of the past as a collection of dusty photos in the attic of the mind, a bundle of old letters [...] But the past was never over."

Emma Gonzalez

AMERICAN

"We are children who are being expected to
act like adults, while the adults are proving
themselves to behave like children."

1999 –
Gun-control Activist

On 14 February 2018, not long before the end of the school day, Emma González found herself among a group of students crouching on the floor of the auditorium of Marjory Stoneman Douglas High School, as a nightmare scenario unfolded around them. A former student, armed with a semi-automatic rifle, had entered the school and opened fire. In under seven minutes, he'd killed seventeen students and staff members, and injured seventeen more. Emma and her friends watched the story unfold on their phones as they hid for more than two hours until armed police escorted them out of the building.

What was supposed to be just another Valentine's Day at school had turned into a nightmare. But this was not the first mass shooting in the United States or even in an American school. It wasn't even the first one that year.

Emma and her friends believed no one should have to go through what their classmates experienced and just days after the shooting, Emma stood at the front of a gun-control rally and gave a speech that was heard across the world. She demanded that the US government introduce stricter gun control laws, so that mass shootings stop happening.

Working together, Emma and her friends organized the March for Our Lives protest, which saw millions of people across the world rally for change on 24 March 2018. Emma continues to campaign for gun reform.

> **One thing you can do:** speak out about issues that affect you, no matter what your age.

1990 –
Actress | Model | Activist

Emma Watson was born in Paris but moved to Oxfordshire, UK, when she was little after her parents separated. Even at six years old, Emma knew she wanted to act, and enjoyed singing and dancing in school productions. Emma got her first professional role when she was nine years old in *Harry Potter and the Philosopher's Stone*. This film would become the first in what was to become a blockbuster series of eight films based on the Harry Potter books.

Work on the Harry Potter films was exhausting, but Emma and her fellow stars also put a lot of effort into their schoolwork, often studying as much as five hours a day with a tutor on set. Because of this commitment, Emma did brilliantly in her GCSEs and A-Levels and went on to get a degree from Brown University in the US.

As well as being an actress, Emma has modelled for Burberry, Lancôme and other major brands. Excited by the idea of using fashion as a tool to alleviate poverty, Emma has developed an ethical clothing range with People Tree.

Emma loves to read and started a feminist book club called Our Shared Shelf to encourage other people to discover some of her favourite books.

Throughout her career, Emma has spoken on behalf of women's rights around the world and in 2014 she was appointed UN Women Goodwill Ambassador.

> **One thing you can do:** stand up for equality, in everything you do.

Emma Watson

BRITISH

"When, at fifteen, my girlfriends started dropping out of their sports teams because they didn't want to appear 'muscly'. When, at eighteen, my male friends were unable to express their feelings. I decided that I was a feminist."

Emmeline Pankhurst

BRITISH

"We are here, not because we are law-breakers;
we are here in our efforts to become law makers."

1858 – 1928
Activist

Emmeline Pankhurst grew up in Manchester, the daughter of two political activists who encouraged her to get a good education. Even though Emmeline was very intelligent, she did not go to university because most universities didn't admit women at that time. Instead she went to finishing school in Paris. On her return, Emmeline married Richard Pankhurst, a supporter of women's rights who encouraged Emmeline to set up an organization that helped married women get the vote. In 1889, she founded the Women's Franchise League.

When her husband died suddenly, Emmeline was left a single mother of four children and became even more acutely aware of how important voting rights were for women. She founded the Women's Social and Political Union (WSPU) in 1903. The WSPU or 'suffragettes' as they were nicknamed by the press, was a women-only organization that campaigned for women's suffrage. Emmeline, alongside her daughters Sylvia and Christabel, ran the WSPU like an army at war with the British government.

She gave speeches encouraging her members to break windows, set fire to empty buildings and chain themselves to railings, to inconvenience the men in charge and draw attention to their cause. Emmeline Pankhurst went to prison many times for her actions and encouraged members of the WSPU to do the same. She died in 1928, shortly before women in the United Kingdom were granted full voting rights.

> **One thing you can do:** continue the fight for gender and racial equality.

1907 – 1954
Artist

Frida Kahlo was born in Mexico where she lived with her family in a blue house. When Frida was a little girl she got a disease called polio, which made her very sick. After nine months in bed and in pain, Frida recovered but was left with a disability that made one leg much thinner than the other. She tried to build up strength in her weak leg by taking part in sports, but no matter what she did, one leg still looked different from the other. Frida often tried to hide this fact by wearing long skirts or lots of pairs of socks.

Frida worked hard at her studies because she wanted to be a doctor. This was not to be. At eighteen Frida was in a bus accident, which left her in a lot of pain and forced her give up the idea of studying medicine.

To distract herself from the pain while recovering in bed, she began to paint and discovered she was very good. In spite of the darkness in Frida's life, she led a life as bold as the colours in her paintings. As her skill grew, so did her fame and soon she had her own studio. Her art gave her many opportunities – Frida travelled the world to visit galleries and attend exhibitions, and she also became involved in politics.

Over the course of her life, Frida would have more than thirty surgeries. She poured this pain into her paintings, more than fifty of which are of herself. After her death, the blue house of her childhood was turned into a museum.

One thing you can do: get to know yourself. Try drawing a picture or writing a poem about the person you are right now, so that you can look back on it in years to come.

Frida Kahlo

MEXICAN

"I am my own muse, I am the subject I know best. The subject I want to know better."

Geraint Thomas

BRITISH

"Everyone in the world of cycling knows how much it is a team sport as well as individual."

1986 –
Cyclist

Geraint Thomas' first bike was a mountain bike with buttons that made noises. When he grew up, he swapped his mountain bike for a blue racer and joined the local cycling team in Wales. Geraint trained hard, winning competitions and eventually earning himself a place at the famous British Cycling Academy.

Geraint has broken bones, torn his spleen and endured painful training rides, often in places far from home. Through all of this, he has persevered. Geraint eventually realized his dream – winning six world cups and two world championships, and achieving Olympic gold medals in both 2008 and 2012.

But even Olympic gold medals and an MBE in 2009 weren't enough for Geraint. His ultimate dream was to win the Tour de France. He got his chance in the 2018 Tour when his teammate Chris Froome lost time in two crashes leaving Geraint as the team's best chance of securing victory.

Geraint, who had ridden more than 3,000 kilometres (1,864 miles) with a broken pelvis in 2013 to help Chris to victory, was now the leader. Chris and the rest of Team Sky were riding to help *him* win. With his team's help, Geraint pedalled to victory becoming the first Welshman ever to win the Tour de France.

One thing you can do: join a team or club to learn the joy of working together to pursue a dream.

1960 –
Artist

Grayson Perry grew up in a working-class family in Essex. When he was four, his father left. Grayson took comfort by retreating into an imaginary world with his teddy bear, Alan Measles.

When Grayson was thirteen years old he confessed to his diary that he thought he might be a transvestite because he liked to wear women's clothes – but he kept this a secret from people.

Grayson did well at school until he was fourteen when the troubles he had growing up made schoolwork difficult. Grayson's art teacher saw his love of the imaginary world and encouraged Grayson to go to art school where he was able to express himself in different mediums. He was also then able to reveal to people that he was a transvestite and he liked to dress in women's clothes.

After art school, Grayson moved to London where he took an evening class in ceramics. The work from his class sold well. Encouraged by this, Grayson worked harder, incorporating aspects of his life into his pieces, including his teddy bear, Alan Measles, and his female alter ego, Claire.

Today, Grayson's ceramic work – as well his tapestry and prints – sells for tens of thousands of pounds and has been displayed in exhibitions all over the world. Grayson won the 2003 Turner Prize, a visual arts prize for British artists.

One thing you can do: experiment with ways to express yourself artistically.

Grayson Perry

BRITISH

"My mistakes make my style."

Hamdi Ulukaya

KURDISH

"You have to get involved. You have to raise your voice and you have to take a stand. We can't solve all the problems, but we have to make sure that we stand for something."

1972 –
Businessman | Philanthropist

Hamdi Ulukaya grew up in Turkey, herding sheep to make cheese and yoghurt with his Kurdish family. He went to school to study to be a teacher but left before he had finished his education. Hamdi became involved in political organizations that spoke up for the rights of Kurdish people who had suffered from persecution in Turkey and throughout the Middle East.

Hamdi moved to the United States to study. His father suggested that he should start a cheese factory. It was hard at first and Hamdi worried a lot about how he would be able to pay his employees each month, but he persevered.

In 2005, Hamdi saw a sales listing for a yoghurt factory. He took out a small business loan and bought the factory. He called his company 'Chobani', which means 'shepherd'. At this time, Greek yoghurt made up about 2% of all the yoghurt sold in the US – today, Greek yoghurt makes up over 50% of the market and much of that is due to Hamdi's company. Chobani now makes and distributes yoghurt all over the world.

Hamdi believes that employers have a responsibility to look after their employees. He pays good wages and gives employees shares in Chobani. Hamdi speaks up for the rights of workers and refugees, and has pledged to donate the majority of his wealth to refugee causes.

One thing you can do: take what you know and think about how you can make it work for you, and how it can potentially help others.

1988 –
Model | Activist

When **Hanne Gaby Odiele** was growing up she felt different from her friends. She had lots of doctors' appointments and surgeries her friends didn't have. This made her feel like something must be very wrong with her.

It wasn't until Hanne was seventeen that she discovered that there was nothing 'wrong' with her. Not long after she was born, her doctors had discovered that despite looking like a typical baby girl she did not have ovaries or a uterus. Instead she had internal testicles that produced male hormones, which her body converted to female hormones.

Hanne was born intersex. The surgeries Hanne had as a child were to 'correct' what was thought to be something wrong with her.

Shortly after her discovery, Hanne started modelling and connecting with other intersex people on social media. She hoped that modelling would give her a platform to tell her story and to help other intersex people. Hanne achieved this dream, appearing on the cover of *Vogue* and modelling for fashion houses such as Prada, Chanel and Vera Wang.

Hanne disagrees with what happened to her – as a child she was unable to consent to the irreversible surgeries, and Hanne believes that her parents had not been fully informed of the consequences. Hanne believes that she and other intersex people weren't born 'wrong' – it's just that society has the wrong idea of what gender should be.

> **One thing you can do:** accept the ways you are different to other people and the ways other people are different to you.

Hanne Gaby Odiele

BELGIAN

"I want to tell young intersex people that you can be beautiful and you can be successful no matter what you do."

Hefina Headon

BRITISH

"We intend to keep the support group going so that we can help people in trouble in the communities, that's our intention. There are others who also need our help."

1930 – 2013
Human Rights Activist

Hefina Headon grew up in a mining town in South Wales. After her first marriage came to an unhappy end, she married her childhood friend, John, a miner and taxi driver. Hefina had a thyroid disorder and diabetes, but despite this, she was very active in the community – she fundraised for the YMCA and attended Labour Party campaign meetings. She became known as 'Mrs Hellfire' due to her fiery attitude and stubbornness.

Between 1984 and 1985, miners all across Britain went on strike, angry at the government's plans to close down hundreds of coal mines. Hefina threw herself into protesting, picketing outside the mines with the workers. She was contacted by Lesbians and Gays Support the Miners (LGSM), a group that was raising money to help those out of work during the strike. Even though some of the miners were against it, Hefina welcomed LGSM into her community. She recognized that miners and the gay community had a common cause – both groups were being attacked by society.

The miners lost the battle, but Hefina showed her support for LGSM by travelling to London to march at Gay Pride in 1985. For the rest of her life she was a powerful voice for human rights. In times of great hardship, Hefina brought hope and positivity to a community.

One thing you can do: stand up for the rights of others, whatever their background or beliefs.

1939 –
Actor | LGBTQ Activist

Ian McKellen was born in Burnley, UK. He loved going
to the theatre and dreamed of becoming an actor, so he auditioned
for school plays and joined a local theatre group. Even in these early
performances, audiences could see he was very talented.

At eighteen, he earned a place at Cambridge University where he
performed in more than twenty plays. After university, Ian went on
to become one of the world's greatest actors appearing in plays,
television programmes and blockbuster films. Some of his most
famous film roles include Gandalf in *The Lord of the Rings* trilogy and
Magneto in the X-Men series. In 1991, Ian received a knighthood for
his services to the performing arts.

Ian is gay, a fact he didn't speak about openly until 1988 when the
UK government introduced a piece of legislation called Section
28. This prevented local authorities from promoting homosexuality,
forbidding them from saying that being homosexual is normal
and should be accepted. Ian helped set up an organization called
Stonewall to campaign against the government's plans and to lobby
for lesbian, gay, bisexual and transgender equality.

Ian and the other cofounders of Stonewall succeeded and Section
28 was repealed in 2003. Today, Stonewall continues to campaign for
equality and for the rights of people in the LGBTQ community.

One thing you can do: read about how members of the
LGBTQ community have been discriminated against in
the past and present. Stand with your LGBTQ friends
in stopping discrimination and inequality.

Ian McKellen

BRITISH

"Nothing though is more important than to continue to enable young people to have a voice, their own voice: to empower themselves and their kind, however they define themselves."

Ibtihaj Muhammad

AMERICAN

"It's important to me that youth everywhere, no matter their race, religion or gender, know that anything is possible with perseverance."

1985 –
Fencer

When Ibtihaj Muhammad was growing up she liked to play with dolls. But she didn't have one that dressed like her. Her family were Muslim and believed that women and girls should cover their hair by wearing a hijab. Ibithaj remembers wrapping small pieces of tissue around her dolls' heads to make them dress like she did.

Ibtihaj's parents wanted her to play sports, but wanted to find sports that would allow her to dress in a way that fit with their Islamic faith. One day, Ibtihaj's mother saw someone fencing and thought the headdress, sleeved jacket and trousers made it the perfect sport. So when Ibtihaj was thirteen she signed up for the school team.

Ibtihaj loved fencing. She trained hard and earned a scholarship to college, then a place on the US Olympic team.

At the 2016 Olympic Games Ibtihaj won a bronze medal in the team sabre competition. She became the first female Muslim to win a medal for the United States.

Ibtihaj has since started a clothing company with her siblings to make clothes that are both fashionable and in keeping with Muslim beliefs. She is a sports ambassador for the US government and to celebrate Ibtihaj's achievement, the company that makes Barbie dolls released a doll of Ibtihaj that comes complete with her own hijab and sabre.

One thing you can do: ditch the label. Help others understand that gender, religion and skin colour are not obstacles to achieving dreams.

1986 –
Animal Rights Activist

When **James Aspey** was seventeen he was diagnosed with a type of cancer called leukaemia and told that he only had six weeks to live. Thankfully James received treatment and after three years, he was cancer free.

James became a personal trainer to try and help other people be healthy. He met a man who suggested that James try being vegetarian. In 2012, James tried this as an experiment for seven days. During this time he began to look into the health benefits of cutting animal products from his diet, as well as how animals were treated in modern farming. James loved the health benefits and hated what he discovered about animal mistreatment so his experiment stuck.

Now James is vegan, and campaigns for animal rights and peace over violence. During his campaigns he has committed to a year's vow of silence and cycled from Darwin to Sydney, a distance of over 5,000 kilometres (3,106 miles), to show how fit a person living on a vegan diet can be.

James has a successful YouTube channel, which he uses to promote his campaigns as well as the benefits of the vegan lifestyle. He is a successful public speaker and has given talks about his journey to audiences all over the globe.

> **One thing you can do:** learn more about what you choose to eat. Does it make you healthier or less healthy? Does it do good in the world or bad?

James Aspey

AUSTRALIAN

"You have to get involved. You have to raise your voice, and you have to take a stand. We can't solve all the problems, but we have to make sure that we stand for something."

Janelle Monae

AMERICAN

"Embrace what makes you unique,
even if it makes others uncomfortable."

1985 –
Singer | Actress | Activist

Janelle Monáe was always eager to take part in local talent shows while she was growing up in Missouri, US. Both of her grandmothers played the organ and she would sing with them while dreaming of one day becoming a star.

When Janelle finished high school, she got a place at the American Music and Drama Academy in New York. Money was tight and she had to fund her studies by working as a maid. Although Janelle worked hard she felt out of place in New York; as if she was learning how to sound and act like someone else. She wanted success, but she wanted to be herself, too.

Janelle moved to Atlanta, where she was able to surround herself with musicians and artists, and experiment with her own sound. Janelle performed whenever she could. Hearing her sound, the band OutKast asked her to perform on several of their tracks.

Soon, appreciation for her unique style spread and Janelle became a star just like she dreamed she would be, but on her own terms. Janelle produces music on her own label Wondaland and uses her platform to speak out against police brutality, gun violence and sexism.

One thing you can do: stay true to yourself – you don't need to change who you are in order to achieve something great.

1990 –
Entrepreneur | Creator | Humanitarian

Growing up with his single mother in the French countryside, Jérôme Jarre was a quiet but happy child. He'd always wanted his own business, so at nineteen, Jérôme set off first to China, then to Canada to launch start-up companies. Sadly, his businesses weren't successful, so in 2013 he bought a one-way bus ticket to New York.

In the Big Apple, Jérôme started posting funny videos to social media app, Vine. His silly pranks and signature smile soon went viral and he was invited onto *The Ellen Show*. From there, his followers on Vine and then Snapchat snowballed, until millions of people were watching his videos every day.

Jérôme decided to use his influence as a force for good. In 2017, he posted a video about the drought in Somalia where thousands of people were facing starvation. He asked his followers to donate money for those in need, starting the movement Love Army for Somalia. Within twenty-four hours, the movement raised $1 million and organized a plane to fly sixty tonnes of food to Somalia.

Jérôme's Love Army continues to do amazing work, most recently raising money in Myanmar for the Rohingya refugee crisis. Jérôme has brought millions of people together and shown that social media can really make a difference.

> **One thing you can do:** use social media to inspire change. Take part in a charity fundraising challenge or share a vlog about an important issue close to your heart.

Jerome Jarre

FRENCH

"Everyone is looking for a purpose in life [...]
We are always wondering why we're here.
But I've learned that we have to create
that purpose for ourselves."

Jim Yong Kim

KOREAN-AMERICAN

"You have to set a really difficult target and then have that really difficult target change the way you do your work."

1959 –
Anthropologist | President of the World Bank

Jim Yong Kim was born in Seoul, South Korea. His family moved to the United States when he was five. Jim did well in school and then studied to become a doctor before moving on to study anthropology.

His interests in medicine and in people across the world inspired him to start an organization called Partners in Health. The ambitious aim was to bring modern medicine to the poorest people in the world by training people within those communities to become medical professionals.

The success of Partners in Health was noticed by the World Health Organization (WHO) who hired Jim to work as an advisor. At the WHO he aimed to increase the number of people in Africa receiving HIV medication by six times in just two years. This difficult target was missed but the aim was achieved in four years – still far sooner than it would have been had the target been more conservative.

In 2012, Jim became president of the World Bank. His bold aim was to eliminate extreme poverty by 2030. Jim's work in developing countries had allowed him to see some of damage the World Bank had done in the past – Jim was once even in favour of shutting the bank down. But instead he took on the challenge of refocusing the bank's work to invest in healthcare, infrastructure and projects to improve the everyday lives of people in the developing world.

> **One thing you can do:** dream big. Reach for the impossible in order to change the way you go about getting what you want.

1974 – 2016
Politician | Activist

When JO COX was a girl in Batley, Yorkshire, UK, she and her granddad would talk together about the people in their town. Jo was always interested in helping people and she devoted her life to doing just that.

Jo was the first member of her family to go to university. While at Cambridge, Jo felt lonely and like she didn't fit in among some of the other students who were more privileged than she was.

After university, Jo worked for a Labour MP in the Houses of Parliament and then in the European Parliament. She spent ten years working at British aid agency, Oxfam, working with people in places such as Darfur and Afghanistan.

From her charity work, Jo saw what happened to people when problems in the world were ignored. She wanted to change things and ran for election to the Houses of Parliament to represent her local constituency, Batley and Spen. She won.

While in Parliament, Jo helped chair a group dedicated to helping the people of Syria and was a member of groups working towards improving the lives of people in Palestine and Pakistan, as well as her home county, Yorkshire. She also campaigned to raise the issue of loneliness as one affecting many people around the UK.

Sadly, Jo was assassinated on the steps of Birstall library where she was working to serve the area in which she had grown up.

> **One thing you can do:** look out for loneliness in the people around you and take some time to have a chat.

Jo Cox

BRITISH

"We are far more united and have far more in common with each other than things that divide us."

Jonnie Peacock

BRITISH

"I try not to have disappointments, because a lot of the bad things that happen in life teach you things."

1993 –
Athlete

When Jonnie Peacock was five years old he had a disease called meningitis that damaged the muscles in his right leg so badly that it had to be amputated.

Despite having lost his leg, Jonnie longed to play football just like his hero David Beckham. He told his doctor this when he was being fitted for a prosthetic leg, so his doctor sent him to a Paralympic sport talent day. It turned out that Jonnie had talent, lots of it, and more importantly than that, Jonnie had the will to win.

Jonnie was a very fast runner, and the more he trained the faster he got. In 2012, he was ready to compete in international competitions. Over his career so far, Jonnie has won six gold medals in the 100 metres sprint, and has won gold at both the World Para Athletics Championships and the World Para Athletics European Championships.

Jonnie was the first amputee Paralympian to compete on *Strictly Come Dancing* and was invited to Buckingham Palace to receive an MBE for his services to athletics.

> **One thing you can do:** when bad things happen, think about what you can learn from them and how the experiences will make you stronger.

1996 –
Political Activist

Joshua Wong was born about eight months before the UK government handed control of Hong Kong back to China on the understanding that China would allow the people of Hong Kong to elect their leaders democratically. As Joshua grew up he became aware of how China was breaking this promise.

Joshua began protesting when he demonstrated against a planned rail link. In 2011, he co-founded a student activist group called Scholarism. The group encouraged young people to protest against the Chinese government's refusal to allow democratic elections. Joshua organized a protest in which 100,000 fellow activists took part, even though many of them were too young to vote.

In 2014, Joshua organized and took part in what became known as the Umbrella Movement – a pro-democracy protest that saw thousands of people camping out on the streets of Hong Kong. This resulted in parts of the city being shut down for seventy-nine days.

Joshua's work has upset the Chinese government, and he has been imprisoned on multiple occasions. But even in prison he will not be silenced – despite strict prison discipline Joshua is determined to keep fighting.

In February 2018, Joshua and the Umbrella Movement were nominated for a Nobel Peace Prize for their peaceful efforts to bring about political reform in China.

One thing you can do: fight for your future. You may be young, but your voice matters so speak up to make sure you are heard (as long as it's safe to do so where you are).

Joshua Wong

CHINESE

"They can lock up our bodies, but they cannot lock up our minds."

J. K. Rowling

BRITISH

"We do not need magic to change the world,
we carry all the power we need inside ourselves
already: we have the power to imagine better."

31 July 1965–
Writer

Growing up in the south of England, things weren't always easy for **Joanne Rowling**. Her mother was very sick with a disease called multiple sclerosis and she didn't get on well with her dad. Joanne finished writing her first story when she was six, and did well at school, earning a place at university to study French.

Joanne came up with the idea for her most famous book when she was stuck on a train from London to Scotland. When she got back to her flat in Edinburgh she started writing about a boy who went to wizard school. Once she had finished her manuscript, she sent it to many publishers, but it was rejected. Joanne persisted and finally a publisher agreed to publish *Harry Potter and the Philosopher's Stone*.

To date, her books for children have sold 450 million copies and have been translated into eighty languages. The Harry Potter books have been made into a blockbusting movie series, as well as a theme park. Her crime thrillers for adults, written under the name Robert Galbraith, have also been phenomenally successful.

Joanne uses her fame as a platform to speak about issues that matter to her, such as mental health. She supports a number of charities and has two of her own. Volant awards money to help women and children living in poverty in Scotland, and Lumos aims to help end the need for orphanages around the world by 2050.

One thing you can do: use what power you have to stand up for people who have less than you.

1954 –
Children's Rights Activist

On his first day of school, **Kailash Satyarthi** saw something that would set him on the path towards his life's work. He saw a boy sitting with his father outside the school mending shoes. When he asked the boy's father why the boy was doing this instead of going to school, he was told that some children were born to work. Kailash could not accept this.

When Kailash grew up he qualified as an electrical engineer and became a teacher, but he never forgot about the boy outside the school gates. In 1980, he left teaching to start an organization that worked to free children working in slave-like conditions. The organization sent in undercover operatives to discover where children were being held and then led raids to free them.

Kailash campaigned to make education a right for all Indian children and also to make child labour illegal. In 1998, he organized the 80,000-kilometre Global March Against Child Labour, which lasted almost six months. Now it is a worldwide network of trade unions that seeks to eliminate all forms of child labour and ensure access for all children to good-quality public education.

Kailash's work has not only changed laws – it has changed the lives of thousands of children. He was awarded the Nobel Peace Prize in 2014, sharing the prize with Malala Yousafzai (see page 116).

> **One thing you can do:** don't take your education for granted – use it to fight for the right of other children to attend school.

Kailash Satyarthi

INDIAN

"I dream for a world which is free of child labour,
a world in which every child goes to school.
A world in which every child gets his rights."

Kofi Annan

GHANAIAN

"The world today spends billions preparing for war; shouldn't we spend a billion or two preparing for peace?"

1938 – 2018
Diplomat | 7th Secretary-General of the UN

When Kofi Annan was at boarding school in Ghana he believed he learned one of the most important lessons he would ever learn: that the suffering of people anywhere concerns people everywhere.

After winning a scholarship to study in the United States and completing his education, Kofi began his career at the United Nations. This career would lead him to work across the world, eventually becoming the first black African Secretary-General of the UN with the unique position of helping to maintain and promote world peace.

Many questioned whether Kofi, who was softly spoken and friendly, would be suitable for such a commanding job. But he believed in using his diplomacy to persuade world leaders. His methods were proven to work when, in 1998, he managed to persuade a war-mongering Saddam Hussein to allow UN observers into parts of Iraq previously off-limits.

After serving two terms as Secretary-General, Kofi left the UN to set up the Kofi Annan Foundation – a non-profit organization promoting sustainable development, peace and security. Kofi also continued his diplomatic work, and in 2008 was invited by the Ghanaian president to mediate in a Kenyan electoral dispute. He succeeded and persuaded the rivals to agree to a power-sharing government. In 2012, as UN envoy, he persuaded Syrian President Assad to agree to a ceasefire.

One thing you can do: work for peace by talking to your friends and family about important issues.

1984 –
Technologist | Feminist | Activist

Kristen Titus grew up in North Carolina, US, with her three brothers. She studied art history at university, then moved to New York. From a young age, she loved technology and quickly found a job in the industry. She worked for several companies, all of them with a vision to empower people through technology.

Less than a quarter of the technology industry's workforce is made up of women – Kristen wanted to address why girls weren't moving into an area that promised to be one of the highest paying and fastest growing of the future.

She became executive director of Girls Who Code, a company dedicated to introducing teenage girls to computer science by building classrooms inside tech companies and hosting summer schools. Girls can immerse themselves in technology, learning everything from robotics to web design.

Now working for the City of New York, Kristen leads the Tech Talent Pipeline initiative, helping the city's technology industry to grow and ensuring that it is made up of a diverse, balanced and brilliant workforce. Her dream is to see more women in positions of power in technology companies – and she's doing all she can to make this dream a reality.

> **One thing you can do:** join a computing club at school or at your local library, or take an online course – even if you think it's not your thing you might find that you love it.

Kristen Titus

AMERICAN

"Imagine what the world will look like when these women are in the field in equal numbers, building the newest, life-changing innovations. I can't wait."

Lawrence Ferlinghetti

AMERICAN

"Freedom of speech is always under attack
by fascist mentality, which exists in all parts
of the world, unfortunately."

1919 –
Publisher | Poet | Painter | Activist

Lawrence Ferlinghetti grew up in France.
He finished school in New York before going to college, where he surrounded himself with people who were passionate about books.

After serving in the US Navy during World War Two, Lawrence studied in Paris before moving back to the US. He found that he disagreed with the literary establishment's view of the role of art and books – he felt that art should be accessible to all people, not just to highly educated intellectuals. With this in mind, in 1953 he co-founded a bookshop in San Francisco: City Lights Bookstore. In 1955, City Lights started publishing books as well as selling them.

In 1956, City Lights' publication of Allen Ginsberg's *Howl & Other Poems* led to Lawrence's arrest for printing and selling indecent material. Lawrence won the court case that followed, a triumph for freedom of speech that established a precedent for the publication of controversial work with redeeming social importance.

City Lights press soon became known as a publishing house that published books unlike anything the world had seen before. These works were part of a counter-cultural literary movement we now know as the Beat Generation.

Lawrence is also a writer of fiction, a playwright and a painter. *A Coney Island of the Mind* is one of the bestselling volumes of poetry written by a living US poet.

One thing you can do: defend freedom of speech wherever possible. Read as much as you can.

1907 – 1977
Photographer | Model | War Correspondent

Lee Miller grew up in New York and had a very difficult childhood.

At the age of nineteen, disaster almost struck Lee when she was nearly hit by a car in New York. Thankfully, she was saved by the owner of a group of magazines that included *Vogue*. He recognized Lee's potential as a model and she became an overnight sensation.

But Lee soon got tired of posing for photographers. She wanted people to pose for her. She moved to Paris where she trained with the artist Man Ray, working as his apprentice, eventually returning to New York and setting up her own studio.

Lee loved Europe and soon returned. When war broke out in 1939, she was hired by *Vogue*, not to model but to be their war correspondent. She was one of a handful of female war correspondents, and took pictures of the London Blitz, the Liberation of Paris and the devastating scenes inside concentration camps. She even took photographs inside Hitler's abandoned home and had her picture taken in his bath.

After the war, Lee settled into life in a farmhouse in Sussex, UK, which was often filled with her famous artist friends. Her son didn't become aware of his mother's incredible achievements until after her death.

One thing you can do: don't be pigeon-holed – strive to achieve your dreams even if people think you could be better at something else.

Lee Miller

AMERICAN

"I would rather take a photograph than be one."

Leyla Hussein

BRITISH-SOMALI

"My activism comes from this curiosity and my fierce determination to protect my daughter."

1980 –
Psychotherapist | Gender Rights Activist

When **Leyla Hussein** was seven years old she was subjected to a tradition known as Female Genital Mutilation (FGM). It wasn't until years later when Leyla had her own daughter that she began to question what had happened to her.

Leyla believes that FGM is child abuse, and should be treated as such, with the people guilty of organizing and performing it being sent to prison for their crimes. But that is not what happens. FGM has been illegal in the UK for more than thirty years, yet not a single successful prosecution has been brought, despite estimates that 6,500 girls are at risk of FGM within the UK every year.

Determined to change this, Leyla set up Daughters of Eve – a non-profit organization that supports women and girls and raises awareness on FGM. She also created the Dahlia Project, to provide support for victims of FGM and to help break the cycle of FGM within families.

Leyla appears regularly on radio and television and gives talks to raise awareness. Speaking out has not been easy but Leyla is determined to continue despite the risks.

One thing you can do: learn more about FGM and speak with your family and classmates about it.

1887 – 1976
Artist

Laurence Lowry started drawing lessons when he was eight years old and living in a leafy suburb of Manchester. He received a good education but financial difficulties meant his family had to move to the industrial town of Pendlebury. At first, Laurence didn't like Pendlebury and the factories that belched smoke up into the sky. But when he started to draw and paint them, he began to see everything differently.

In his early twenties, Laurence took a job as a rent collector. It meant he had to walk all over the city. He painted what he saw – pictures of real life in an industrial landscape. He painted after work and at the weekends, taking evening classes where he studied under French artist Adolphe Valette. Laurence was inspired by French Impressionists such as Dante Gabriel Rossetti, but developed a style that was all his own.

Laurence became very successful. In 1968, he turned down a knighthood that he was to be awarded in recognition for his work. He never married or had children – when he died he left all of his works to a woman who shared his surname and had written to him saying she was interested in becoming an artist. He is considered one of the greatest artists of the twentieth century. Despite his success in art he continued his job as a rent collector, a job he held for over forty years.

One thing you can do: look for beauty on your doorstep. L. S. Lowry was one of the first artists to see beauty in the industrial landscape. Where will you find it?

L. S. Lowry

BRITISH

"I worked to get rid of the time, even now I work for something to do. Painting is a wonderful way of getting rid of the days."

Maeve Higgins

IRISH

"I have this feeling that I missed the day in school where they explained how to live your life."

1981 –
Comedian | Writer | Activist

Maeve Higgins had a happy childhood, growing up in a big family in Country Cork, Ireland. She'd spend hours climbing trees, picking fruit and baking with her siblings. She loved to read and would tell funny stories to anybody that would listen. When she was nine, the family moved to Zimbabwe for her father's work. For the first time, Maeve experienced a way of living that was very different from the one she'd known in Cork.

After a couple of years, Maeve moved back to Ireland. As she grew up, she still loved telling funny stories and was able to start making a living as a stand-up comedian. Maeve built a successful career in Ireland, performing, writing for newspapers and even creating a TV series with her sister, Lilly. But soon Maeve wanted a change, so she moved to London and then New York, taking on the comedy scenes there.

Now settled in New York, Maeve presents the popular podcast 'Maeve in the United States: Immigration IRL' where she talks to other immigrants about their experiences of moving to the US. She wants to share their stories with the world, discovering why they left their places of birth and what happened once they reached the US. She uses the podcast to shine a light on the issues facing immigrants today.

One thing you can do: talk to people about their lives – particularly older people. They might not have been able to share their stories before.

1989 –
Politician | 122ⁿᵈ Lord Mayor of Sheffield | Activist

There are a lot of things that make Magid Magid a bit different from the average Lord Mayor, not least that he chose music from *Star Wars* for his inauguration and that his official picture features him squatting on the marble balustrade of the town hall.

Magid was born in Somalia not long before the outbreak of civil war. Fearing for the safety of her son and daughter, Magid's mother took her family on a long and dangerous journey to a refugee camp in Ethiopia before moving to Sheffield, UK. In Sheffield, Magid learned English and worked hard at school, while his mother supported the family as a cleaner. Times were tough, but Magid was a good student and earned a place at Hull University.

After university, upset by the anti-immigrant outlook of the UK Independence Party, Magid joined the Green Party, where he rose through the ranks before becoming a candidate for city councillor.

Charming and popular, the council elected Magid to be the city's youngest ever mayor. Although he was well-liked as a member of the council, not everyone was happy to see a 'black Muslim immigrant' hold the office, and he received hateful letters. But even this Magid took in his stride, inviting some of the letter writers to a round table where they were able to discuss their concerns.

Magid's unorthodox inauguration picture became an Internet sensation and his historic appointment has made him famous all around the world.

> **One thing you can do:** don't be afraid of having uncomfortable conversations. Speaking to people who don't agree with you can help change minds.

Magid Magid

(Magid Mah)

BRITISH-SOMALI

"You could be the most racist person to me; I will
still open that door for you. You can't solve hate with
hate. That doesn't solve anything whatsoever. I will
still be kind to you, because at the end of the day
you're human; we all go through the same problems,
same issues, face the same things, and I believe
people can come around just by meeting people."

Malala Yousafzai

PAKISTANI

"Let us pick up our books and our pens,
they are the most powerful weapons."

1997 –
Activist | Writer

Malala Yousafzai spent the first few years of her life growing up in a beautiful part of Pakistan called Swat. Life was good for Malala until groups of armed men, who were members of an extremist political group called the Taliban, began making attacks on girls' schools. These men believed that girls did not have a right to an education and should stay at home.

Malala was angry – she liked going to school and didn't think anyone should take that away from her. Instead of staying home, Malala spoke out about what was happening. Even though she was just twelve years old, Malala gave speeches about what was going on and even had her own blog on the BBC. To stay safe, she wrote her blog under a false name, but her cover was blown in 2009. Even though this put her in great danger, Malala refused to give up.

But the Taliban wanted to stop her. On 9 October 2012, members of the group boarded Malala's school bus and shot her in the head.

Miraculously – she survived. Malala was flown to the UK where she made a full recovery. In 2014, she was awarded the Nobel Peace Prize – but her fight isn't over. She continues to campaign for the rights of women and girls, writing bestselling books and giving talks all over the world.

One thing you can do: don't take your education for granted. Around the world, millions of children cannot go to school, including about thirty-one million girls.

1962 –
Writer

Malorie Blackman had worked her way through the children's books in her local library by the time she was eleven years old. When her parents split up two years later, Malorie coped by inventing fantastical worlds in her head.

Malorie did brilliantly at school and dreamed of becoming an English teacher so she could help other children discover the joy of books. But her teacher didn't give her a reference to study English at university – instead she said that black people became secretaries, not teachers.

When Malorie left school she studied to become a computer programmer. Her career allowed her to travel all over the world, but Malorie still loved stories. She enrolled on a creative writing course, where she was encouraged her to share her work. Malorie's first book was published when she was twenty-eight and she hasn't stopped writing since.

Now Malorie is a bestselling, award-winning children's author. Malorie wanted her readers to meet characters from all kinds of backgrounds, and many of her books feature a central character of colour.

In 2013, Malorie became the Children's Laureate, a role dedicated to helping young people develop a love of books and reading.

> **One thing you can do:** visit your local library and pick up a book about a character from a different background to you.

Malorie Blackman

BRITISH

"Reading is an exercise in empathy;
an exercise in walking in someone
else's shoes for a while."

Manal al-Sharif

SAUDI ARABIAN

"I believe a society will not be free if the women of that society are not free."

1979 –
Women's Rights Activist

One day, Manal al-Sharif stood at the side of the road in Saudi Arabia trying to hail a taxi. Men driving past jeered at her. Manal became frustrated – she owned a car and knew how to drive it, but Saudi law forbade her from doing so. Driving a car may not sound like a big deal, but Saudi Arabia has very strict laws. Women must be with a male guardian when they go out, or have written permission. They can't wear certain clothes, play some sports or swim in public.

In 2011, Manal posted a video of herself driving a car on YouTube. It got more than 700,000 views in one day. Manal was imprisoned for 'driving while female'. Manal's small act of defiance caused her to lose her job and custody of one of her children. It also forced some of her family members to leave the country for their own safety.

But Manal didn't give up. Instead, she set up a website called Miles4Freedom to help her campaign and penned a bestselling book. Thanks to the efforts of activists like Manal, Saudi Arabia lifted the ban on women driving in June 2018. Days before the ban was lifted, many activists were jailed, including Manal's friends. She was due to fly home to Saudi Arabia and drive as soon as the ban was lifted, but did not make the trip due to the arrests. For these women, there is still a long way to go before equality in Saudi Arabia is achieved – but Manal won't give up the fight. She continues to campaign for women's rights around the world.

One thing you can do: ask the female drivers in your family to pledge the miles they drive to Miles4Freedom, calling an end to male guardianship in Saudi Arabia.

Physicist | Chemist | Feminist

A little girl called Maria Skłodowska was curious to discover more about the world around her. After doing well in school, Marie wanted to carry on studying – but at the time, only men were allowed to go to university in Warsaw, Poland. She dreamed of going to a university in Paris, where girls were admitted, but she didn't have enough money. So, Marie made a deal with her sister, Bronya, who also wanted a degree. Marie would work as a tutor and governess, supporting her sister financially. In return, Bronya promised to help Marie with her university fees once she had graduated.

In Paris, Maria changed her name to Marie and discovered her love for science. She married a man, Pierre Curie, who shared that love. Together, they investigated a newly discovered element, known as uranium, and the radiation it produced. Marie's curiosity and determination led her to discover two new radioactive elements in the periodic table, one she named polonium after her homeland, and the other she named radium. Marie published more than thirty papers on the properties of these new elements, and in 1903 she won the Nobel Prize in Physics with her husband. After Pierre's death she was awarded the 1911 Nobel Prize in Chemistry. Marie Curie was the first woman to win a Nobel Prize and the first person to be awarded two.

Marie discovered that X-rays could be used to diagnose patients. She helped to develop portable X-ray machines and, during World War One, she was even known to drive these machines to soldiers on the frontlines, helping to save the lives of over one million people.

> **One thing you can do:** investigate the world around you – read books, watch programmes or do online research to discover how things work.

Marie Curie

FRENCH-POLISH

"Be less curious about people and more curious about ideas."

Marley Dias

AMERICAN

"Frustration is fuel that can lead to the development of an innovative and useful idea."

2005 –
Activist | Writer

As a little girl Marley Dias loved to read, but was frustrated that most of the books on her school reading list were about white boys and their dogs. Marley wanted to read books that featured people that looked like her, and not just as sidekicks but as main characters. She believed that books featuring characters of colour must be out there somewhere. She was determined to find them and make it easier for everyone else to access them too.

Marley launched a campaign called #1000blackgirlbooks in order to collect 1,000 books with black girls as their central character to donate to communities around the United States. People rose to the challenge and collected more than 10,000 books. Marley even had the opportunity to add her own book to the pile when she landed a publishing deal.

Marley may have found her books, but the world still needs more. A study showed that just 8.4% of books published in the US in 2016 featured an African-American as a main character and the numbers were even lower for people of Latino, Asian Pacific and Native American descent. In 2017, of the 9,115 children's books published in the UK, just 1% had a black or minority ethnic main character. Marley continues to work to change this, speaking at events and sharing her story.

One thing you can do: demand diverse books. Speak to your librarian about stocking books that feature diverse characters in main roles. If they can't help, start a campaign like Marley.

1956 –
Tennis Player | Activist

From a young age, Martina Navratilova would pick up a tennis racket and practise hitting the ball against a wall. Her mother and grandmother had both been good players and Martina followed in their footsteps, training regularly from the age of seven. Martina won her first national championship when she was fifteen. Around this time, influential people in the tennis world started to notice how good she was – but there was a problem. Martina lived in what was Czechoslovakia, now the Czech Republic, a country under the control of the Soviet Union, which made travelling and competing difficult.

Determined to compete, Martina made the heartbreaking decision to defect to the United States in 1975. Defecting meant she was cut off from her family for many years, but it allowed her to train with some of the world's best coaches. Martina became the most successful female tennis player in the world and won an enormous fifty-nine grand slam titles between 1974 and 2006.

And it wasn't just on the court that Martina showed her courage. She was one of the world's first openly gay sports figures, speaking out about her sexuality at a time when very few people did. Today Martina is still active in tennis, commentating and coaching. She supports a number of charities, many of which provide help for the LGBTQ community.

One thing you can do: show your support for female athletes by going to watch a women's sporting event.

Martina Navratilova

CZECH-AMERICAN

"People in the States used to think that if girls were good at sports their sexuality would be affected. [...] The image of women is changing now. You don't have to be pretty for people to come and see you play. At the same time, if you're a good athlete, it doesn't mean you're not a woman."

Mary Beard

BRITISH

"When it comes to silencing women, Western culture has had thousands of years of practice."

1955 –
Classicist | Feminist | Broadcaster

Mary Beard grew up in Shropshire, UK, and was always fascinated by history. At school she was good at Latin and loved going to the British Museum to look at artefacts from the ancient world. She even earned pocket money during summer holidays by helping out on archaeological digs.

While she was studying at Cambridge University, Mary found that many male students and staff members had a negative view of how well women could do in the academic world. This surprised Mary and spurred her on; she was awarded a first-class degree and became a Professor of Classics. As a professor, Mary had the opportunity to inspire her students to love history as much as she did.

Mary began making documentaries and writing books, helping to bring the ancient world to life for new audiences. Her documentaries are insightful and well-liked – but she is not popular with everyone. A male newspaper critic once commented that Mary wasn't glamorous enough to be on television. This hurt Mary, but she hit back by saying that she looked like an ordinary woman and was proud to be showing girls who watched the programme that they didn't have to have surgery or dye their hair to appear on television.

Mary continues to speak out and promote the idea that women of all ages working in academia and television deserve respect.

> **One thing you can do:** watch a programme presented by a female academic, or read a book written by one.

1921 – 2005
Mathematician | Engineer

Mary Jackson grew up in Hampton, Virginia, US. She was a brilliant mathematician and enjoyed solving all kinds of problems and equations. After school, she went to university to study mathematics and physical science.

In 1951, Mary joined what was then known as the National Advisory Committee in Aeronautics, later renamed the National Aeronautics and Space Administration (NASA). There Mary worked as a 'human computer', doing calculations for early space programmes. Mary was so good that a fellow engineer, a white man named Kazimierz Czarnecki, encouraged her to train to become an engineer. Almost all of the other engineers were white and male, like Czarnecki, but Mary was determined.

Because of segregation laws, she had to get special permission from the local government to study alongside white students. In some parts of the US at the time, segregation meant people of colour had to go to separate schools, sit in different areas of restaurants, buses and cinemas and even use separate public toilets to white people. Mary got permission to study and her hard work paid off. In 1958, she became the first black female engineer at NASA.

Even after conducting important research at NASA for many years, Mary was frustrated that there weren't more people like her working there. She moved to become the Federal Equal Opportunity Specialist with a view to hiring women from different backgrounds and developing their careers.

> **One thing you can do:** do some research to discover other important figures in history – dig a little deeper into the stories you are familiar with and see if you can find some forgotten heroes or heroines.

Mary Jackson

AMERICAN

"We have to do something like this to get them interested in science. Sometimes they are not aware of the number of black scientists, and don't even know of the career opportunities until it is too late."

Mary Prince

BRITISH

"The man that says slaves be quite happy
in slavery – that they don't want to be free –
that man is either ignorant or a lying person.
I never heard a slave say so."

1788 – 1833
Abolitionist | Writer

Mary Prince was born to enslaved parents on the island of Bermuda. When she was a child, she was sold to a new 'owner' and taken away from her family.

In 1826, Mary married former slave Daniel James, but her owner was angry that Mary had wed a free man and didn't want her husband living on his land. He made life difficult for Mary and in 1828, she was separated from her husband and taken to London.

While in London, Mary was employed as a paid house servant by abolitionist Thomas Pringle, founder of the Anti-Slavery Society, and given a place to live in his home. Pringle was moved by Mary's story and arranged for her to tell it to a biographer named Susanna Strickland. Together they wrote *The History of Mary Prince, A West Indian Slave, Related by Herself*. The book was published in 1831.

People were appalled by what they read. Mary's story shared what it was like to be an enslaved human being, forced to work in the colonies of the British Empire. The book was reprinted three times in its first year and was used in the campaign to abolish the slave trade. In 1833, slavery was abolished in Britain, making it illegal to buy or sell human beings. Despite this, estimates suggest there are still tens of thousands of people living in modern slavery in the UK today.

One thing you can do: never take your liberty for granted. Talk to an adult about how you can support freedom of others and find out more about modern slavery.

1944 –
Politician | 7th President of Ireland | Lawyer

Mary Robinson was the only girl of five siblings – and that wasn't the only way she stood out. Mary's family were Catholic, but she decided to study law at Trinity College in Dublin at a time when many disapproved of Catholics attending what was thought of as a Protestant university. At twenty-five Mary stood out again when she became Ireland's youngest ever law professor.

In 1969, Mary was elected to the upper house of the Irish Legislature, a post she would be re-elected to for the next twenty years. In that role, Mary championed human rights causes, including lobbying to relax restrictions on contraceptives and to reform the law on homosexuality in Ireland.

In 1990, Mary stood once again, this time running for president. She won and became the first ever female president of Ireland. She continued to speak out for human rights and was one of the first to visit Somalia during the famine in 1992 and to visit Rwanda after the genocide in 1994. At the end of her presidency, Mary was appointed United Nations High Commissioner for Human Rights, a role in which she visited countries where people's rights were at risk of being violated and helped to improve monitoring.

Mary now runs her own non-governmental organization, the Mary Robinson Foundation – Climate Justice, which stands up for the rights of those most likely to be affected by climate change.

One thing you can do: hold politicians accountable for what they say they aim to do by writing letters to your local council.

Mary Robinson

IRISH

"Human rights are inscribed in the hearts of people;
they were there long before lawmakers drafted their
first proclamation."

Massimo Bottura

ITALIAN

"Using the spotlight that you have to make
the invisible, visible is very important. But my
dream would be 'normality' – for it to be normal
to open a soup kitchen like [the Refettorio], full of
art, of beauty, rebuilding people, fighting waste,
involving all the community of chefs."

1962 –
Chef | Philanthropist

Massimo Bottura became interested in cooking as a boy while watching his mother and his grandmother prepare delicious meals to feed the family. When he left school, Massimo trained to become a chef, travelling the world and learning in some of the most famous kitchens. The hours were long, but Massimo paid attention, trying to hone all the skills he would need in order to become a talented chef and one day open his own restaurant.

Massimo's hard work paid off and he became a famous chef, writing cookbooks and opening a Michelin-starred restaurant in Modena, Italy.

In 2012, two earthquakes hit Massimo's home town of Emilia-Romagna, Italy. During the disaster 360,000 wheels of cheese were damaged, which was terrible news for the region's cheese industry. But Massimo devised a recipe that used lots of the cheese. So many people wanted to try his delicious dish that every one of the damaged wheels was sold.

Massimo now operates a non-profit organization called Food for Soul that aims to tackle world hunger and food waste. Today it is estimated that one-third of all food produced is thrown away, while 800 million people around the world are undernourished. Massimo wants to rectify this by forming community kitchens called 'Refettorios', where chefs work to use food going to waste to serve hungry people.

One thing you can do: avoid wasting food by only buying as much as you need. Talk to a responsible adult about sharing.

1928 – 2014
Writer | Civil Rights Activist

When **Maya Angelou** was three years old, her parents separated from one another. Maya and her older brother were sent to live with their grandmother in Arkansas, US. Here, Maya's uncle taught her to read and she discovered a love of books that would have a great impact on her life.

Maya and her brother returned to live with her mother in St Louis when she was seven, but it wasn't a happy homecoming. Maya was sexually abused by her mother's boyfriend. She built up the courage to tell her mother what had happened – and the man died not long after. Maya believed that telling her mother had caused his death so she didn't speak to anyone other than her brother, Bailey, for five years. She believed that if she spoke, something very bad would happen.

At school, Maya was encouraged to read plays and poetry by her teacher. Through this literature, Maya found her voice again. She became a talented singer and actress as well as a civil rights activist working alongside Malcolm X and Martin Luther King Jr.

In 1969, Maya published her first autobiography *I Know Why the Caged Bird Sings* which became a world-wide bestseller. Maya wrote many bestselling books including her autobiography series and spoke up for the rights of African-Americans and women throughout her life.

One thing you can do: write a poem with a positive message to inspire others.

Maya Angelou

AMERICAN

"I've learned that people will forget what you said, people will forget what you did, but people will never forget how you made them feel."

Meghan Markle

AMERICAN

"With fame comes opportunity, but it also includes responsibility – to advocate and share, to focus less on glass slippers and more on pushing through glass ceilings."

1981 –
Activist | Duchess of Sussex

Meghan Markle grew up in California, US, with her African-American mother, a therapist and yoga instructor, and her white father who worked in television. One day at school she was asked to fill out a form and tick a box to say whether she was black, Hispanic, white or Asian. Meghan didn't know what to do, so she didn't tick a box. When she asked her dad about it, he said that next time she should draw her own box. Meghan has been doing that ever since.

When Meghan was eleven, she saw an advert that implied only women should do housework. Meghan wrote a letter to the company behind the ad, as well as influential women across the United States like Hilary Clinton, to point out the sexist implications. Because of her campaign, the advert was changed.

When Meghan grew up she followed her dream of becoming an actress, but found it tough to find roles – casting directors would tell her she was too black for white roles and too white for black ones. But she didn't give up, and eventually landed the perfect role in a show called *Suits* which became a smash hit.

Today she finds herself in a new role. In 2018, with the world watching, Meghan married Prince Harry and became the Duchess of Sussex. Meghan uses her platform to draw attention to issues such as modern-day slavery and mental health problems.

> **One thing you can do:** draw your own box – don't let other people define you. Do things because you want to do them and not because people expect you to do them.

1969 –
Actor | Activist

Growing up in Port Talbot, Wales, **Michael Sheen** dreamed of becoming a professional footballer. He was offered a place on the Arsenal youth team aged twelve, but had to turn it down because his family couldn't make the move to London.

Michael was a strong performer on the pitch and, in his teens, he discovered he was a talented performer on the stage too. He joined the National Youth Theatre of Wales and went on to attend the prestigious Royal Academy of Dramatic Arts in London.

Michael was soon landing roles on stage and screen, but this award-winning actor never forgot the opportunities he was given growing up.

The steelworks in Port Talbot used to be the biggest in Europe, but over the last few decades many employees have lost their jobs, due to cuts. Michael now uses his fame to help draw attention to the neglect of industrial communities such as Port Talbot, working to ensure people are given fair access to opportunities and the encouragement to pursue their ambitions, like he did.

Michael still uses his football skills too, regularly competing in charity tournaments to raise money for UNICEF, an organization he became an ambassador for in 2014.

One thing you can do: take every opportunity that is given to you and make the most of them so that one day you might be able to offer opportunities to others.

Michael Sheen

BRITISH

"The only thing you can really change is you."

Michaela DePrince

SIERRA LEONEAN-AMERICAN

"Never be afraid of living and loving."

1995 –
Ballet Dancer

When **Michaela DePrince** was little, no one could have predicted that she would grow up to be a ballet dancer. Born in war-torn Sierra Leone as Mabinty Bangura, her father was killed by rebels and her mother died from fever and starvation. Mabinty was taken to an orphanage where the women who were supposed to care for her taunted her for her vitiligo, a skin condition that causes lighter patches on her skin. One day, she came across a magazine that would change her life forever. The front cover featured a picture of a ballet dancer. Mabinty decided that somehow she would grow up to be a dancer, too.

Mabinty was adopted by an American couple, along with another little girl, also called Mabinty. The pair moved to the United States and were renamed Michaela and Mia. Here, Michaela's adoptive mother supported her daughter's desire to dance, and enrolled her in classes. Michaela worked hard and took dancing very seriously. She strove to overcome all barriers, from her own self-consciousness to racial prejudice.

Michaela's hard work paid off. She debuted professionally at the Joburg Ballet in South Africa and appeared on *Dancing with the Stars*. Aged eighteen she joined the Dutch National Ballet where she still dances. Along with ballet, Michaela is passionate about reaching out to disadvantaged children. She is a War Child ambassador and encourages people all around the world to work hard, strive for what they want and dare to dream.

One thing you can do: don't be scared to follow your dreams, no matter how far-fetched they feel. Work hard towards your goals.

1964 –
Lawyer | 44th First Lady of the United States

Michelle Obama was born Michelle LaVaughn
Robinson in Chicago, US. Michelle's mother and father did not have
a lot of money, but they taught Michelle and her brother the value of
hard work. Michelle took their advice on board – she could read by
the age of four and graduated school with top grades.

Michelle kept on working hard through college and got an advanced
degree from Harvard Law School. After graduating, Michelle got a
job at a law firm that served her community. While working there she
was asked to supervise a new intern, Barack Obama.

Michelle and Barack Obama married in 1992 and had two children.
Barack became President of the United States with Michelle at his
side. Michelle served as First Lady for eight years and was the first
African-American First Lady.

As First Lady, she planted a vegetable garden at the White House
with volunteers from local schools and visited schools across
the country to encourage children to get a good education. Michelle
also started a campaign to tackle childhood obesity with her
Let's Move! campaign.

One thing you can do: stay away from negative people.
Surround yourself with people who help you to work hard
and achieve your goals, and lift them up in return.

Michelle Obama

AMERICAN

"One of the lessons that I grew up with was to always stay true to yourself and never let what somebody else says distract you from your goals."

Mikaila Ulmer

AMERICAN

"If only one person saves the bees, it won't really do much good. But if you get the whole village and you get everybody to help chip in and do just a little bit to help save the bees, you can save the bees so quickly. It's just taking something, from me to we; you can get it faster and get it better and you can get more, which is really amazing!"

2004 –
Entrepreneur | Conservationist

When Mikaila Ulmer was just four years old, two things happened that would change her life forever. Firstly, her great-grandmother gave her an old cookbook which had a recipe for lemonade in it. Secondly, she was stung by a bee twice within the same week.

Being stung made Mikaila scared of bees, but her mother suggested that Mikaila research the insects to try and better understand them. Mikaila was fascinated by the lives of these tiny creatures and also sad to find out that bees were under threat.

Mikaila wanted to do something to help – she had the brilliant idea of making lemonade sweetened with honey from local bees, inspired by her granny's recipe. Mikaila began selling her delicious lemonade, and soon she was supplying her local pizza restaurant.

When Mikaila was nine, she appeared on the television show *Shark Tank* and secured a $60,000 investment. With this money and the contacts she'd gained from the show, she was able to grow her business, Me & the Bees. Now her lemonade is stocked in supermarkets and restaurants across the United States. For each bottle of Me & the Bees Lemonade sold, money is donated to organizations fighting to save honeybees.

One thing you can do: learn more about bees and the small things you can do to protect them, like planting bee-friendly flowers, buying local honey and asking your parents to avoid using pesticides in the garden.

1982 –
Ballet Dancer | Public Speaker

When she was a little girl, **Misty Copeland** would make up dance routines to songs by her favourite singer, Mariah Carey. Misty and her family moved around a lot, so even though dance was her passion, she wasn't able to go to lessons. Unlike most ballet dancers, who start lessons almost as soon as they could walk, Misty didn't take a ballet class until she was thirteen years old.

But starting late didn't stop Misty. She was a natural and within a matter of weeks of her first lesson she was ready for pointe shoes, something most ballet dancers train for years to achieve. Soon Misty was dancing in front of big audience and voted the best young dancer in Southern California. Misty began training with the American Ballet Theatre where she became the first African-American soloist in over twenty years, and the only African-American principal dancer in the company's seventy-five year history.

Misty found it tough being one of the only African-American dancers in the company and wants to make it easier for others. She and the American Ballet Theatre have set up Project Plié – an initiative to increase ethnic representation in the United States' dance companies by ensuring students with diverse backgrounds get the resources and support they need.

One thing you can do: experience is great, but don't let not having any stop you from trying new things. Starting last does not mean you can't get ahead and finish first.

Misty Copeland

AMERICAN

"You have to be the one promoting yourself.
If you don't think that you're worthy,
you're never going to make it."

Mo Farah

BRITISH

"It doesn't just come overnight, you've got
to train for it and believe in yourself;
that's the most important thing."

1983 –
Athlete | Philanthropist

Born in Mogadishu, Somalia, Mo Farah moved to the UK when he was eight. When he started school, one of only two English phrases he knew was 'Come on then!', but after saying this earned him a black eye on his first day, he learned the language as quickly as he could. That wasn't all Mo did quickly – he was nicknamed 'Ferrari' because he was such a fast runner.

Mo wanted to use his speed to become a football player, but his PE teacher thought he would make a great distance runner. He was right – in 2001 Mo won the European Junior Championship for the 5,000 metres.

On 4 August 2012, Mo electrified the crowd at the London Olympics by becoming the first British man to win gold in the 10,000 metres, only to wow them again, winning gold in the 5,000 metres. Could he do the same at Rio in 2016? Mo hoped so, but it almost didn't happen. During the 10,000 metres he tripped and fell – but Mo picked himself up and crossed the finish line first. He became the first man to win gold in both the 5,000 and 10,000 metres in two consecutive Olympic games, a feat which earned him a knighthood for his services to athletics.

In 2017, Mo retired from the track, but didn't stop running. Mo's sights are now set on marathons. He won the 2018 Chicago Marathon, setting a new British record.

One thing you can do: put in the practice – whether it's playing the piano, studying for exams or training for a sport. Hard work now leads to results and achievement in the future.

1942 – 2016
Boxer | Activist | Philanthropist

Muhammad Ali was born Cassius Clay in Kentucky,
US. When Cassius was twelve years old someone stole his bike. This made him very angry. He joined a local boxing club so that if he ever found out who took it, he would be able to beat them up. But his initial motive of beating up the bike thief was soon forgotten.

Cassius soon started entering competitions and winning. He trained hard and got better and better, beating more opponents as time went on. In 1964, he became the World Heavyweight Champion.

That same year, Cassius converted to Islam and changed his name to Muhammad Ali. Muhammad's faith was very important to him – his love of peace meant he felt unable to fight in the Vietnam War when he was called to serve in 1967. Refusing to serve was an offence and Muhammad was sent to prison and stripped of his boxing titles.

In 1971, Muhammad appealed to the Supreme Court to have his convictions overturned. He won this court case, but that couldn't change the fact he had lost four years of training and competing. Ali had to work hard to get back to the position he had formerly held, but his hard work paid off and in 1974, he reigned as World Heavyweight Champion once again. To this day, he is considered one of the greatest and most influential boxers of all time.

One thing you can do: believe in yourself. Set high standards and have confidence in your abilities to achieve them.

Muhammad Ali

AMERICAN

"Impossible is just a big word thrown around by small men who find it easier to live in the world they've been given than to explore the power they have to change it. Impossible is not a fact. It's an opinion. Impossible is not a declaration. It's a dare. Impossible is potential. Impossible is temporary. Impossible is nothing."

Muhammad Yunus

BANGLADESHI

"Poverty does not belong in civilized human
society. Its proper place is in a museum.
That's where it will be."

1940 –
Economist

Muhammad Yunus was born in Bangladesh, the third of fourteen children. After doing well at his village school, Muhammad went on to university and won a scholarship to study in the United States.

At university, Muhammad became fascinated by economics and how money flowed through communities. In 1974, famine ravaged much of Bangladesh. Muhammad realized that the people affected by famine needed access to money, but not from traditional money lenders that charged enormous interest rates and huge penalties for people unable to pay. They needed loans from a reliable lender – loans of small amounts that could be used to start businesses. These small businesses would make enough money to pay back the loan but would also lift communities out of poverty.

Muhammad began by lending small amounts of his own money and seeing what happened. The loans were used to help start or grow small businesses and, as they were all paid back in full, he gave out more loans. His loans became Grameen Bank.

Banks like Muhammad's have been set up in more than one hundred countries all over the world and have lent money to millions of people. These banks form part of a new movement with the aim of helping some of the world's poorest people lift themselves out of poverty.

> **One thing you can do:** look for small ways to fight poverty. Encourage your parents to buy fairly traded items that don't rely on unfair employment practices.

1999 –
Refugee Ambassador

Muzoon Almellehan grew up in a quiet neighbourhood, surrounded by friends. Her life was full of promise until, when she was fourteen, civil war broke out and tore her homeland of Syria apart. Muzoon had to flee her home with her family, able only to take what belongings she could fit into a small backpack. Of all her most cherished possessions, Muzoon chose to take her school books because, even though they were heavy, she knew that if she lost her education she would lose everything.

Muzoon and her family found themselves in a refugee camp among thousands of others, with no electricity or Internet. The camp had a school which Muzoon attended but few other girls did. When Muzoon investigated why, she discovered these girls were being married off by their parents, in the hope that marriage would offer them some protection. But Muzoon believed the best thing for these girls, and for the future of Syria, was for them to get an education. After lessons finished each day, Muzoon went from tent to tent encouraging people to send their daughters to school.

Soon people started to take notice, not just her fellow refugees but also organizations such as UNICEF who helped her to spread the message to more people. At nineteen, Muzoon was appointed the youngest ever Goodwill Ambassador to the UN.

After three years in the camp, Muzoon and her family moved to Newcastle where she hopes to attend university.

> **One thing you can do:** use your voice. Speak out about issues you care about in any way you can – to your friends, teachers and online. Don't wait to be told your voice matters, show people that it does.

Muzoon Almellehan

SYRIAN

"Education is power. Education is the future. Education makes us who we want to be."

Nelson Mandela

SOUTH AFRICAN

"Do not look the other way; do not hesitate.
Recognize that the world is hungry for action,
not words. Act with courage and vision."

1918 – 2013
Politician | 1st President of South Africa | Activist

When Nelson Mandela was born he was named Rolihlahla, but was given the name 'Nelson' on his first day at school by his teacher, Miss Mdingane. When Nelson was growing up, South Africa was under a system known as apartheid, which gave all the power to white South Africans. Black South Africans were restricted in where they could live and what jobs they were allowed to do. Nelson saw that this was unfair and wanted to change things.

He went to university to study law and met many others who wanted to end apartheid in South Africa, too. Nelson became the leader of a group of activists. At first, they tried to protest against the government peacefully, but when this did not work they resorted to bombing property, though they were always careful that nobody was hurt. The South African government responded by arresting Nelson Mandela and locked him away in prison for a life sentence. Throughout that time, world leaders put pressure on South Africa to end apartheid, allow free elections and to release Nelson.

Nelson was released from prison in 1990. After his release, he continued to work to end apartheid and in 1994 he became president of South Africa marking the start of a new era for the country.

One thing you can do: around the world, thousands of people are wrongfully imprisoned. Seek out petitions calling for their release.

1982 –
Boxer

Nicola Adams wasn't a typical tough girl growing up – she had asthma and was small for her age. Nicola's parents were often fighting and her father was violent towards her mother. They separated when Nicola was eleven and, though things were happier at home from then on, her mother had to work two jobs to support the family while Nicola looked after her brother.

Nicola struggled at school and had trouble concentrating. After she was diagnosed with attention deficit hyperactivity disorder (ADHD), she found an escape at her local gym where she tried boxing. In 1996, the Amateur Boxing Association of England lifted its 116-year ban on women boxers and Nicola decided she was going to be one of the very first superstars.

When Nicola was a teenager, her mother became very ill with meningitis and almost died. Again, Nicola had to look after her brother and support her mother, doing the washing, cleaning and shopping alongside her boxing classes. Her mother made a full recovery and was able to be there for Nicola as she became a stronger and stronger boxer. She was also there to support her daughter when Nicola told her she was bisexual.

Nicola's determination in the boxing ring saw her win tournament after tournament, taking gold at the Olympics in 2012 and 2016. Boxing has brought a lot of opportunities Nicola's way – she has walked the catwalk in a suit inspired by her hero Muhammad Ali and has been awarded both an MBE and an OBE for her services to the sport.

> **One thing you can do:** try a boxing or self-defence class to relieve stress, get strong and maybe take your first steps to winning a gold medal.

Nicola Adams

BRITISH

"I want to [...] become the greatest amateur boxer in British history. And nothing is going to stand in my way."

Nikesh Shukla

BRITISH

"Diversity shouldn't need to be celebrated. It should be inherent. Normal. The usual. Not a thing we notice, positively or negatively."

1980 –
Writer | Diversity Activist

Nikesh Shukla grew up in Harrow, North London. He had a passion for language and wanted to be a rapper. He started writing in his mid-twenties and soon had several novels under his belt, along with regular columns in national newspapers.

Nikesh's own career may have been going well, but when he heard a World Book Night list announced that didn't contain any works by black, Asian, or minority ethnic writers, Nikesh felt he had to do something. Together with a publisher, Nikesh crowdfunded enough money to launch a book called *The Good Immigrant*, a collection of essays about what it is like to be a person of colour in Great Britain. The book was a huge success and sold more than 60,000 copies.

By making the book, Nikesh had created a platform for BAME writers to share their stories and experiences – but it wasn't enough. He wanted there to be more opportunities for these writers.

Nikesh teamed up with his literary agent to make that happen, starting a new literary agency with the aim of finding, encouraging and promoting the work of writers underrepresented in mainstream publishing, including BAME, working class, LGBTQ and disabled writers.

One thing you can do: start a magazine, blog or vlog and encourage diversity by inviting collaborations from people from different backgrounds.

1952 – 1979
Community Leader | Activist

Olive Morris was born in Jamaica, but moved to Brixton, South London, when she was nine. In the 1960s and 70s, times were difficult for people of colour living in areas like Brixton. They often faced discrimination when looking for work or housing, and could even be attacked by racist groups such as the National Front. These communities were offered little protection from the police, who also discriminated against them, stopping and searching anyone who looked 'suspicious'. For some police officers it seemed that being black was enough to make a person 'suspicious'.

Olive could see the injustice of these laws. In her early teens, she joined an activist group called the British Black Panther Movement and founded the Brixton Black Women's Group, campaigning for education, better living conditions and an end to repression.

Despite having left school with no formal qualifications, Olive earned a place at Manchester University where she studied economics and social sciences. In Manchester, Olive helped to found another activist group, and stood up for people in her community including those who, like herself, lived in squats.

Tragically, Olive died of cancer aged twenty-seven. Though Olive was very young when she died, her work touched the lives of many in her community and a building and garden in Brixton have been named after her.

One thing you can do: enquire in your local library about community volunteering opportunities for young people. If there aren't any initiatives at the moment, why not start one?

Olive Morris

BRITISH

"My heart will always be in Brixton."

Oskar Schindler

GERMAN

"I knew the people who worked for me. When you know people, you have to behave towards them like human beings."

1908 – 1974
Industrialist | Humanitarian

Before World War Two, Oskar Schindler had tried his hand at many trades. When war broke out, he seized the opportunity to earn money on the black market. In 1939, he used these funds to open an enamelware and ammunitions factory in Kraków, staffing it with cheap labourers. Due to the political climate in Poland at the time, many of these labourers were Jewish people.

Under the Nazi party, Jewish people were discriminated against, lost their jobs and had their homes and businesses seized. They were beaten in the streets and forced to live in run-down areas of cities called ghettos. Oskar was a member of the Nazi party, but he did not share their views about Jewish people.

In 1942, Oskar could not ignore the sight of Nazis forcing Jewish people into trucks and transporting them to death camps. Desperate to protect his workers, Oskar told the Nazis that they were essential skilled workers. Oskar's factory made bullets for the German army, but Oskar ordered his workers to make sure all of the bullets were defective so that they could not harm anyone.

By 1944 it was clear Germany was losing the war. More and more Jewish people were being taken to camps. To protect his workers, Oskar persuaded the Nazis to let him take his 1,200 essential workers to the Sudeten Land where he had set up a new factory. Oskar spent his entire fortune bribing Nazis to keep his workers safe, until the war ended in 1945.

> **One thing you can do:** when reading a news story, remember that behind every stranger's name mentioned, there is a person with thoughts, feelings, hopes and dreams just like you.

Date of birth unknown
Journalist | Activist

Paris Lees was born biologically male, but she always knew she was a girl. She quickly realized, however, that other people didn't see her the way she saw herself. Paris tried to conform to her family and classmates' expectations by boxing and playing football, but she still didn't fit in and was badly bullied.

At age sixteen, she committed a robbery and was sent to prison when she turned eighteen. She spent time on the vulnerable men's unit and realized just how far off the rails she had come. Once her sentence had been served, Paris knew she needed to turn things around. She went back to college, then moved to Brighton to study English at university where she started identifying as a girl.

Despite sometimes being judged in the street, Paris began to flourish professionally. She worked as a journalist, founding the first British magazine aimed at the transgender community, *META*, and contributing articles to other major magazines and newspapers. Now, Paris presents documentaries on identity and prejudices faced by other minority communities. In 2018, she became British *Vogue*'s first openly transgender columnist in the magazine's 125-year history.

Paris is an inspiring example of a woman who stayed true to herself and had the courage to ignore what people told her she should act like, in favour of doing what was right for her.

One thing you can do: avoid labelling others – let them decide for themselves what gender or sexual orientation they identify as and respect their wishes.

Paris Lees

BRITISH

"I don't need permission to use the label 'woman'. I'm a woman because I say so."

Professor Green

(Stephen Manderson)

BRITISH

"Communication is a big problem with us men.
We don't like to talk about our problems;
we think it makes us look weak."

1983 –
Rapper | Mental Health Advocate

Born and raised as Stephen Manderson on a Hackney estate in London, Professor Green was brought up by his nan. His father wasn't around much and Stephen would sometimes spend hours watching the bus stop opposite his flat, hoping his father would hop off a bus and come to visit. But he rarely did.

Stephen did well in school until, aged around thirteen, he started feeling really anxious. He'd skip lessons and take drugs instead. But Stephen's passion for rap, or 'talking music' as his nan called it, would lead him on to great things. In 2008, he won £50,000 in a rap battle contest, and the following year he was collaborating with superstars like Lily Allen, Emeli Sandé and The Streets on his first album.

After his father took his own life, Stephen started raising awareness about the mental health issues facing people today. Suicide is the biggest killer of men aged under forty-five in Britain, and Stephen is using his voice to try and change this. From presenting award-winning documentaries to openly talking about his own struggle with anxiety, Stephen is making mental health more visible and encouraging people to have those important conversations before it's too late.

One thing you can do: chat to your family about how you're feeling and start conversations with friends who might be struggling to cope.

1907 – 1964
Marine Biologist | Writer | Ecologist

Nature-lover **Rachel Carson** studied marine biology at university, landing a government job in the fisheries department after she graduated. As well as being a skilled scientist, Rachel was a talented writer. In her spare time, she would turn her scientific work into award-winning essays that were published in newspapers and magazines. In 1941, she transformed one of her articles into a book called *Under the Sea Wind*, launching her career as a famous science writer.

She gave up her government role to devote herself to writing full time in 1952. Rachel believed humans were unique in their ability to transform the natural world and was upset by the damage being done by chemical pesticides. Rachel spent four years writing *Silent Spring*, a book that started a national debate about the dangers posed by pesticides.

The book was big news and President John F. Kennedy called on his Science Advisory Committee to investigate. Their findings supported Rachel's. Despite battling cancer, Rachel accepted an invitation to testify before congress. She demanded that the government make new laws to protect people and the natural world. Although Rachel died not long after, her legacy lives on. She is considered one of the most important and influential science writers of the twentieth century.

One thing you can do: ask your parents to avoid using chemical pesticides in the garden and to buy organic foods where possible.

Rachel Carson

AMERICAN

"Future generations are unlikely to condone our lack of prudent concern for the integrity of the natural world that supports all life."

Raif Badawi

SAUDI ARABIAN

"Freedom of speech is the air that any thinker breathes; it's the fuel that ignites the fire of an intellectual's thoughts."

1984 –
Writer | Blogger | Activist

On 9 January 2015, Raif Badawi was led into a square in Jeddah and beaten across the back and legs fifty times by a security officer employed by the government of Saudi Arabia. After he was flogged, Raif was returned to prison.

Raif is not a murderer. He is not a thief. In fact, he is not guilty of anything that would be considered a crime in the United Kingdom. Raif is a blogger in Saudi Arabia, a country where speaking against the government or the religious authorities can be punishable by death.

In 2008, Raif set up a website called Free Saudi Liberals which he hoped would encourage people to discuss religious and political issues in Saudi Arabia. For this, and for allegedly making statements that people of different faiths should be treated equally, he was charged with insulting Islam and was sentenced to ten years in prison, 1,000 lashes and a ten-year ban on leaving the country after his release. Word of his imprisonment spread. Many world leaders condemned the Saudi government for imprisoning Raif and called for his release. So far, his sentence has been upheld, though he has received no further lashes due to poor health.

In December 2015, Raif was given an award from the European Parliament for Freedom of Thought. His wife and children, now living in Canada, continue to campaign for his release.

One thing you can do: visit the Amnesty International website to discover a variety of ways you can join the effort to free political prisoners all over the world.

1982 –
Actor | Rapper | Activist

Riz Ahmed grew up in Wembley, London, in a wealthy British Pakistani family. At school he sometimes felt like he didn't fit in as some of the teachers showed favouritism towards certain white students. At Oxford University he felt like an outsider again, the upper-class, black-tie culture was not his thing at all. In response, Riz started his own club night, bringing the kind of music he loved to Oxford and sharing it with his fellow students.

Riz moved back to London and took his club night to various venues around the city while he attended drama school. Taking the name Riz MC, he released his first tracks and won rap battle after rap battle, before being invited to perform at huge festivals like Glastonbury.

As well as being a talented musician, Riz is an award-winning actor. His breakthrough moment came at age twenty-three when he landed a role in the film *The Road to Guantanamo*, a story about the illegal detention of three young men at Guantanamo Bay. On returning to the UK from a screening of the film in Germany, Riz was illegally detained by airport security who wrongly suspected him of being involved with a terrorist organization, purely based on the fact he was of South Asian descent.

Riz has appeared in a number of other blockbuster films, choosing roles that allow him to challenge some of the cultural labels he has grown up with all his life. Riz writes about some of his experiences in *The Good Immigrant* edited by Nikesh Shukla (see page 164).

> **One thing you can do:** identify what others might label you as and think about how you can transcend that label. How can you stretch the definition of what it is like to be someone like you?

Riz Ahmed

BRITISH

"Life is about transcending the labels people impose on you."

Ryan Hreljac

CANADIAN

"All I had to do was take ten steps from my classroom to get to the drinking fountain and I had clean water. Before that day in school, I figured everyone lived like me. When I found out this wasn't the case, I decided I had to do something about it."

1991 –
Activist

When he was seven years old, Ryan Hreljac was told something by his teacher that would change his life. She told him that in lots of places around the world, people weren't able to get clean water. These people often had to walk for hours to get to water that could be contaminated, causing illness and even death. Like most children in Canada, Ryan had never been more than a few metres away from a clean water supply.

When Ryan got home that day he asked his mum what he could do to change things. He earned money doing chores around the house in the hope that he could raise enough to build a well. He earned $70 in four months but he found out it would cost thousands to build just one well. He started talking to more people about water – at after-school clubs and in lessons, drawing attention to the world's water crisis. Soon, he had raised a lot more than $70 and had enough to build his first well at a school in Uganda. He even got to appear on *The Oprah Winfrey Show*.

Since then, Ryan and his family have set up the Ryan's Well Foundation, raising money to build more than 1,000 wells, providing fresh water to communities all over the world.

> **One thing you can do:** think about how difficult your life would be without access to clean water. Try to use less – turn off the tap while brushing your teeth, take shorter showers and only use what you really need.

1981 –
Tennis Player

Serena Williams began to play tennis when she was just three years old, alongside her older sister Venus. Together they would take lessons from their father who had studied training techniques and coaching practices from books and videos. They trained for hours every day on rundown public tennis courts with potholes and sometimes even missing nets. The girls got so good at tennis that the family moved to Florida where they could learn from professional coaches.

Serena turned professional in 1995, just a year after her sister Venus. A natural athlete and no stranger to hard work, her powerful game overwhelmed her opponents and before long she was climbing up the world rankings. Serena won her first Grand Slam singles title in 1999 and went on to win more than twenty in total, sometimes even against her sister. But she played with her sister too, teaming up with Venus for doubles tournaments. Together, they won gold in the 2008 Olympic Games.

In spite of all her outstanding achievements, Serena has faced criticism for the way she looks, deemed by some journalists to be 'unfeminine', but Serena is proud of her powerful physique. Her strength, confidence and skill give her the edge over other players and have helped her to become a true champion.

> **One thing you can do:** do you go red when you exercise? Do you pull a funny face when you sing? Do you stammer when you speak publicly? So what? Don't let fear of people's criticism stop you from doing things you enjoy.

Serena Williams

AMERICAN

"Think of all the girls who could become top athletes but quit sports because they're afraid of having too many defined muscles and being made fun of or called unattractive."

Shami Chakrabarti

BRITISH

"The fundamental values of a democracy cannot be changed because we are provoked by terrorists."

1969 –
Politician | Civil Rights Activist

When Shami Chakrabarti was twelve years old she saw a horrible news story about a serial killer and thought that the man should be sentenced to death. Her father explained to her what a terrible thing it was to take another person's life, no matter what crime they had committed. Shami started thinking about what justice really meant – this would become the focus of her life's work.

Years later, Shami studied law in London, eventually securing a job as a barrister for the Home Office. Throughout her career Shami continued her pursuit of justice and in 2003 she was appointed director of Liberty, a charity that aims to defend civil liberties and protect the human rights of people around the world. She campaigned against what many people saw as excessive and reactionary anti-terrorist measures that were put in place after members of the Al-Qaeda terrorist organization attacked landmarks in the United States on 11 September 2001.

Shami was appointed to the House of Lords in 2016 and has brought her views to new audiences by penning bestselling books, along with speaking regularly on television and radio.

One thing you can do: be careful of making reactionary snap decisions. Think about your choices and how they will affect others, then make calm considered judgements.

1961 –
Soldier | Public Speaker

Simon Weston grew up in Wales and joined the army when he was sixteen. He served all over the world before being sent to the Falkland Islands where a conflict was raging between Argentinian and British forces.

On 8 June 1982, the ship RFA *Sir Galahad* was bombed, killing forty-eight members of the crew. One of those on board, Simon was lucky to survive, but 46% of his body was seriously burned. Doctors fought to save his life. Eventually, Simon was able to return home but he was so badly disfigured even his mother did not recognize him. He had to have many painful operations to rebuild his face.

Simon's injuries made it impossible for him to serve in the army as he had before – and that was the only job he'd ever known. Simon became depressed. But then he got the opportunity to go on a tour of Australia to help raise money for a children's burns unit. Simon decided to focus on the good he could do by sharing his story.

Simon now dedicates his life to serving others. He has set up a charity for young people in Liverpool, has campaigned on behalf of troops and served on the board of a number of important non-profit organizations. Simon has been the subject of many documentaries and bestselling books and has been awarded an OBE and CBE.

One thing you can do: use your experiences, even your negative ones, to help others. Set yourself small goals each day to achieve something big.

Simon Weston

BRITISH

"I've always been very hopeful but I also know that as long as you've got a good work ethic, almost anything is achievable."

Sonita Alizadeh

AFGHAN

"We each have a tool we can use to make change. Mine is my microphone. What is yours?"

1997 –
Rapper | Activist

Sonita Alizadeh was born in Afghanistan when it was under the rule of the Taliban, but moved to Iran when she was very young. In Iran, Sonita lived with her parents as a refugee and was educated by a charity that worked with undocumented children. She learned karate and how to rap, and even started writing her own songs. Sonita also met Rokhsareh Ghaemmaghami, a documentary maker who started filming her story.

When Sonita was fourteen years old, her mother moved back to Afghanistan and told Sonita that she intended to sell her into marriage. Getting married would mean Sonita would have to give up rap, return to Afghanistan and live with a man she barely knew. Like many of the girls living in the camp, Sonita was angry and devastated that this was to be her future. Fortunately, Rokhsareh stepped in, offering her family $2,000 to buy Sonita some more time. Sonita wrote a song called 'Brides for Sale' and shared it with the world. Her rap changed her parents' minds and drew international attention to the issue of forced marriages.

In 2015, with the help of a US charity, Sonita moved to Washington, DC, US, to finish her education. Sonita continues to fight for the rights of the twelve million girls each year who are married before they turn eighteen.

One thing you can do: listen to the messages in Sonita's music and join her in stopping child marriage by sharing her story with friends and family.

Theoretical Physicist | Cosmologist | Writer

As a little boy, Stephen Hawking enjoyed taking things apart to see how they worked. He even built a computer with his friends who nicknamed him 'Einstein' because he was so good at maths and science.

Stephen studied at Oxford University before moving to Cambridge to work on a PhD in cosmology, the study of the origin of the universe. But Stephen started to notice strange things were happening to his body – he was getting clumsier and would trip up for no reason. He was diagnosed with a rare disease called amyotrophic lateral sclerosis (ALS) which affected his brain and spinal cord. The doctors predicted that Stephen only had a few years to live. To begin with, the diagnosis made Stephen depressed, but then he decided that if he didn't have much time left, he'd better not waste it.

Stephen lived much longer than two years. Though his condition was very limiting, leading him to require an electric wheelchair and lose his speech, he continued with his research, winning many awards and discovering new laws regarding the origins of the universe.

Stephen wanted his work to be understood by everyone. Communicating with the aid of a computer program operated by moving a muscle in his cheek, he dictated his book, *A Brief History of Time*, which became an international bestseller. Stephen went on to write several more critically acclaimed titles and delivered lectures on his work around the world.

One thing you can do: there is rarely a good reason to give up on your dreams – don't let any barriers get in your way, physical or mental.

Stephen Hawking

BRITISH

"My goal is a complete understanding of the universe, why it is as it is and why it exists at all."

Stormzy

(Michael Omari Jr)

BRITISH

"It's not always about convincing your parents of what you want to do, but just saying, 'This is what I'm doing; this is what I love.'"

1993 –
Rapper

Stormzy grew up in South London with his mother, brother and two sisters. His big sister introduced him to grime music and Stormzy loved what he heard. He started rapping when he was eleven years old and begged his sister to take him to a party with decks and a microphone. The first time she agreed he just stood in the corner, but the next time he gathered the courage to perform.

Stormzy honed his talent throughout his teens and became a polished performer, but he wasn't signed to a music label. Lots of people said he couldn't be successful without being signed, but Stormzy proved them wrong – his songs were played on the radio and placed in the charts. Stormzy is now a multi-award-winning rapper who performs all over the world.

In 2018, he used his performance at the Brit Awards to call out Prime Minister Theresa May and the UK government for their lack of response to the Grenfell Tower fire. Downing Street released a statement the very next day.

Stormzy uses his success to further the interests of young black people in the UK, sponsoring scholarships for BAME students to attend top universities. He started #Merky, which began as a record label and now includes an outlet for writers too. He teamed up with book publisher Penguin Random House to create #Merky Books, an imprint that publishes young people's writing.

> **One thing you can do:** write a list of all the people that support you and think of meaningful ways you could thank them.

1969 –
Athlete | Politician | Presenter

Tanni Grey–Thompson was born with a
condition called spina bifida which made walking very difficult, so she had to use a wheelchair from the age of seven. Thanks to the determination of her parents, Tanni was able to go to a mainstream school. Here she became interested in sports, including archery and basketball. One day when she was watching the wheelchair race at the London Marathon, Tanni decided that was what she wanted to do. She was going to become an athlete.

So Tanni began training. The local athletics club only had a grass track, which was difficult for wheelchair users to practise racing on, so Tanni and her teammates would train on the ramps in local car parks. In 1988, Tanni was ready to complete in her first Paralympic Games in Seoul, South Korea. She took home a bronze medal. This was to be the first of a staggering five consecutive Paralympic Games.

Tanni has come a long way since racing around car parks. She's set over thirty world records and won the London Marathon six times. Throughout her career, Tanni has campaigned for people with disabilities to have access to sports. She has been awarded a DBE for her services to sport, appointed to the House of Lords and made a baroness by the Queen.

> **One thing you can do:** encourage your school to set up a sports clubs that is accessible to students with disabilities, like wheelchair basketball or sitting volleyball.

Tanni Grey-Thompson

BRITISH

"Being in the public eye can be pretty hard at times, but I have to remind myself that no one makes me do it – I could leave the House of Lords tomorrow and that would be it. Politics is much more divisive and not always easy to deal with, but the lessons I learned in sport help me deal with some of the more silly things."

Tarana Burke

AMERICAN

"The work is really about survivors talking
to each other and saying, 'I see you.
I support you. I get it.'"

1973 –
Activist

When Tarana Burke was a growing up in the Bronx, New York, she was sexually assaulted by a group of boys in her neighbourhood. Her mother did everything she could to help her recover, suggesting Tarana get involved in the community. Tarana was motivated to become an activist and stand up for other girls in marginalized communities.

Tarana founded JustBe Inc, an organization focused on the wellbeing of women of colour. One day at the centre, a young girl confessed to Tarana that she had been sexually abused by her mother's boyfriend. Tarana wanted to find a way to tell the girl she understood how she felt and that it wasn't her fault, she wanted to say the words 'me too' – but she couldn't find the courage.

Tarana wondered what would happen if other women like her had the strength to stand up and say 'me too', demonstrating just how widespread the experience of sexual assault is. Tarana began using the phrase in her group discussions and on social media.

In October 2017, actress Alyssa Milano asked women on Twitter to use #metoo if they had ever experienced sexual assault or harassment. The response was huge and within just a few weeks #metoo had been used more than twelve million times. Thanks to Tarana and Alyssa, women and girls had a platform to share their stories and shed light on just how massive a problem sexual harassment is, erasing the shame and breaking the silence.

> **One thing you can do:** listen to people when they tell you something bad has happened to them. Support them and encourage them to speak to a responsible adult.

1955 –
Computer Scientist | Inventor | Engineer

As a boy, Tim Berners-Lee loved tinkering with his model railway to learn about electronics. Tim's parents helped develop one of the first commercial computers, so Tim was surrounded by stories of how one day computers could be smarter than people.

At university, Tim studied physics and built a computer from an old television with his friends in his spare time. After graduation, Tim took a job at the European Organization for Nuclear Research where he designed a system to help scientists share their research and data with one another more quickly. He used an old US government system called the 'Internet'.

In 1989, when Tim sent the first message on his new system, he was taking the first steps in creating the World Wide Web. Tim could have made a lot of money from his invention, but instead he made it free for all to access, so that the web could continue to grow. Today, it is estimated that more than half the population of the planet are connected to it.

Tim now works to protect his invention from big corporations trying to spy on its users. He set up the World Wide Web Foundation to protect the human rights of web users and is developing software to give them back their privacy. Tim has been repeatedly listed as one of the most important people of the twentieth century, revolutionizing the way we communicate.

> **One thing you can do:** remember that using the Internet is a lot like walking down a busy street – you wouldn't shout out everything about yourself to strangers on the street, so be careful what you share online, too.

Tim Berners-Lee

BRITISH

"I think, in general, it's clear that most bad things
come from misunderstanding, and communication
is generally the way to resolve misunderstandings –
and the Web's a form of communication –
so it generally should be good."

Tu Youyou

CHINESE

"The work was the top priority so I was certainly willing to sacrifice my personal life."

1930 –
Pharmacologist

Tu Youyou was born in Ningbo, Zhejiang, China. A kind and modest girl, she dreamed of helping others when she grew up. Youyou excelled at her studies, but she had to take a break from school when she caught tuberculosis. Youyou's illness inspired her to go into medical research.

Youyou attended Peking University in Beijing, where she developed an interest in traditional Chinese medicine. In 1955, she earned her degree in Pharmacology. Youyou continued her research on Chinese herbal medicine in the China Academy of Chinese Medical Sciences.

During the Vietnam War, a horrible disease called malaria had claimed the lives of countless soldiers. In 1967, Youyou was appointed to lead 'Project 523', a top-secret government project to find a treatment for malaria. Youyou and her team of researchers learned about folk medicine and remedies described in ancient Chinese medical texts. They discovered a plant called sweet wormwood and managed to extract a substance, artemisinin, which helped battle the malaria parasites in the body. Drugs based on Youyou's research have led to the survival and improved health of millions of people around the world.

Despite not having a medical degree or a PhD, Youyou made one of the greatest scientific discoveries in modern medicine. In 2015, Youyou was awarded the Nobel Prize in Medicine and became the first Chinese woman to win a Nobel Prize.

> **One thing you can do:** learn more about historical methods and practices – you never know when an old idea might lead to a new discovery!

1928 – 2016
Astronomer | Astrophysicist

Growing up in Washington, DC, US, Vera Rubin was fascinated by the stars she could see through her bedroom window each night. She wanted to learn everything she could about them, so she and her father built a telescope from a cardboard tube and she started attending local astronomy club meetings.

Vera went on to study astronomy at university, but when she applied to Princeton to study further, she was told that they didn't admit women to their graduate programme. Refusing to let this stop her, Vera found a place at a different university where she could study the galaxies to her heart's content. She worked with some of the greatest astrophysicists of the moment and was soon making incredible discoveries herself.

Vera's observations and research changed the way people saw space. She discovered that galaxies weren't just made up of stars, but also something called dark matter which was only visible by its gravitational effect on the stars. In fact, galaxies were made of more dark matter than anything else. To begin with, people were incredulous about her discoveries, but eventually her theories were proved true and she won many awards for her work.

Throughout her career, Vera faced discrimination because she was female. Not wanting others to suffer as she had in the future, Vera mentored young women who wanted to follow in her footsteps, helping them find their own place among the stars.

One thing you can do: like Vera, see what stars you can spot out of your window at night. You could borrow or buy a book by an astronomer to learn more about the night sky.

Vera Rubin

AMERICAN

"I would prefer to stay up and watch the stars than go to sleep. I started learning. I started going to the library and reading. But it was initially just watching the stars from my bedroom that I really did. There was just nothing as interesting in my life as watching the stars every night."

Virginia Hall

AMERICAN

"The only way for a woman to get ahead
in the world is to get an education."

1906 – 1982
Spy

Virginia Hall grew up in a wealthy family on a farm in Maryland, US. She dreamed of travelling the world, so after college she set off to Europe to study, learning French, Italian and German along the way.

Virginia decided that she wanted to become a diplomat. She got a job at the US Embassy in Poland and then Turkey, but her dreams were dashed when she accidentally shot herself in the leg in a hunting accident. Her leg had to be amputated below the knee, and the State Department had a strict policy against hiring people with disabilities.

Virginia learned to walk again and moved to Paris where she worked as an ambulance driver during World War Two. But after the Germans invaded, she had to flee to London. Here, Virginia volunteered to serve with the Special Operations Unit and became a spy.

She was posted back to France, where Virginia gathered intelligence about the German army, recruited resistance fighters, helped downed Allied pilots and assisted prison breakouts. Virginia played a vital role in the war effort, despite often being in pain from her prosthetic leg. She was known as 'the limping lady' and considered so dangerous that the German secret service devoted an entire department to uncovering her identity.

For her services during the war, she was given awards from the French, US and British governments.

> **One thing you can do:** if people put an obstacle in your path, find another way to achieve your dreams.

1987 –
Inventor | Engineer | Writer

William Kamkwamba grew up in Malawi, Africa. William loved going to school, but when famine hit the area where he lived, his family could no longer afford to send him. Determined to keep learning, William would borrow books from his local library. One book was about electronics. William became hooked and soon worked out how to make money from fixing his neighbours' electrical appliances.

Using what he had learned, William built a wind turbine from scrap metal and bicycle parts. This turbine was able to produce enough electricity to power four light bulbs and charge his neighbours' mobile phones. His invention meant that his family didn't have to use so much expensive kerosene-generated electricity, but instead could use renewable, clean energy from wind.

People were impressed by William's invention and travelled from far and wide to see what he had created. But William hadn't finished innovating yet – he created a solar-powered water pump to provide fresh drinking water for his village and built more turbines to supply power to more homes.

William's fame spread further. His hard work and ingenuity earned him a place at Dartmouth College, US. He has also written a bestselling book called *The Boy Who Harnessed the Wind.*

One thing you can do: try to use less energy – wear a jumper instead of turning on the heating and turn off lights when you leave a room.

William Kamkwamba

MALAWIAN

In life you can go through many difficulties, but if you now what you want to do, if you can focus, and work, then in the end, you will end up doing it. No matter what happens, if you don't give up, you will still succeed."

TM 577/19

INDEX